CHAUCER'S HOST
UP-SO-DOUN

Chaucer's *H*ost:
Up-So-Doun

Dolores L. Cullen

FITHIAN PRESS · SANTA BARBARA · 1998

Published by Fithian Press
A division of Daniel and Daniel, Publishers, Inc.
Post Office Box 1525
Santa Barbara, CA 93102

LIBRARY OF CONGRESS CATALOGING-IN-PUBLICATION DATA
Cullen, Dolores L., (date)
    Chaucer's host : up-so-doun / Dolores L. Cullen.
       p. cm.
    Includes bibliographical references (p.   )
    ISBN 1-56474-254-7 (alk. paper)
    1. Chaucer, Geoffrey, d. 1400—Characters—Herry Bailly. 2. Chaucer,
Geoffrey, d. 1400. Canterbury tales. 3. Christian poetry, English (Middle)—
History and criticism. 4. Lord's Supper—History—Middle Ages, 600–1500.
5. Chaucer, Geoffrey, d. 1400—Religion. 6. Christianity and literature—
England. 7. Bailly, Herry (Fictitious character) 8. Lord's Supper in litera-
ture. 9. Jesus Christ—In literature. 10. Hotelkeepers in literature. I. Title.
PR1875.H67C85   1998
821'.1—dc21   97-44211
                                                                   CIP

For
Ted, my husband
and
Virginia Hamilton Adair
because they were there for me
from the beginning

Reading should be slow and attentive, laborious, intent on the reward contained in the underlying meaning.

—Bede (eighth century)

CONTENTS

ACKNOWLEDGEMENTS

This book has gone through many processes, many transformations. Contributions of time and interest from Mary Breiner and Michael Fultz produced a version I could confidently offer to Sabrina Wenrick. Her comments and inspiration helped beget the variation which was generously read by Dr. Richard Barnes of Pomona College. His kindness and academic expertise set me in the direction of worthwhile revisions. The Claremont Writers Group, for a time, and ultimately the San Dimas Writers Group must be credited with being patient and encouraging with my many rewrites. And always, in the background, there was the supportive presence of my children.

Preface:
About Chaucer and Me (and You)

WHEN I MET Chaucer for the first time, I was no ingenue. In spite of that, he swept me off my feet. As I read the *Canterbury Tales*, I could feel something developing, but it was an experience I'd never had before. Then, without warning, it quickened. There was no longer any doubt: Chaucer's work had taken up a life in my intellect. It began gesturing to me, teasing me, cavorting along the paths of my mind. I found it irresistible. When it coaxed, I followed where it led. I invite you to join us—the poem and me—in our adventure together. Chaucer's poetry will bilocate with inexplicable ease and be alive to you as well as to me, if you will extend your mind in a gesture of welcome.

My introduction to Chaucer was also my introduction to Middle English. It is the poem in Middle English that captivated me. The language seemed much like an interesting dialect, perhaps a presentation of Scottish brogue. After a short time a pattern of regular differences became evident—*widwe* for *widow*, *arwe* for *arrow*, or *-ynge* for *-ing*. Once I was comfortable with those, and perhaps ten or twenty other patterns, the poetry began to recognize me as a new friend; our time together became delightful exchanges.

The poem proposed a word game, and I accepted the challenge. The Middle English words held many possibilities as they came at me: some were tossed playfully as toys, some lifted as jewels from a treasure trove, some were spheres enclosing whole galaxies, and some pregnant—needing assistance to be delivered of their burden.

There were words that tested whether I was being attentive to the game. A line would speak of a woman "buxom and virtuous," but the poem was just teasing the twentieth-century reader. The image of a very good woman, who is also physically well-endowed (what more could a husband want?) is the wrong image. Chaucer is really saying that she is *obedient* (buxom) and virtuous! So I learned to be careful not to let the poetry put me at a disadvantage.

As I watched the progress of the poem, there were many moments when a word would seem to be going in two directions at the same time: if an object is *curious*, it might be *artistic and costly*, or it might be *magical; prys* can be the *price* one pays, or the *prize* one wins. These moments frequently caused hesitation, and need for deciphering. I wondered if the reader was meant to choose between, or accept both messages.

And then there were topics cut off suddenly with "I need say no more," or "let it go." (I like to refer to these as *vagueries*—meaning, "that which is vague.") Vagueries gave the feeling that the poet wasn't playing fair. Or perhaps, I thought, there must be rules I've never heard about for this game. I knew that allegory was the preferred literary style in Chaucer's day, and that allegory can tell two stories at the same time, the way parables do in the Bible. Sophisticated audiences in the fourteenth century loved allegories, and enjoyed the challenge of discovering their hidden meaning. I must assert that I had no interest in *interpretive* allegory, whose distortions, for example, take a metamorphosis from Ovid and twist it into a Christian exemplum. *Inventive* allegory, written with two—perhaps more—story lines in mind as it is created, was the challenge. So I set my goal on identifying the multilayered images that teased and tantalized my mind's eye.

Words in Chaucer's amazing vocabulary need to be looked at from many points of view. If the poem throws out a word, if the word bumps the reader, bothers him, he mustn't just let it lie there, or toss it back without examination—"I've seen this word before. There is nothing new here."—because then he's forfeited his chance to win the game. (He may continue playing, but he cannot win.) I always asked, "What is odd about this troublesome word?" Sometimes it would be the location; sometimes the spelling; sometimes repetition; sometimes juxtaposition. Each time a word was put into play, I needed to decide on its category—from toy to treasure. How would it fit properly into its surroundings?

❦

The basis of the *Canterbury Tales*, as you may know, is the journey of a fascinating group of pilgrims, from many social levels and backgrounds, who are traveling from London to Canterbury. The travelers are given a night's bed and board in "the Tabard" before they set out. The Host, to whom the Tabard belongs, offers to guide the wayfarers—at his own cost. This is important information that we'll deal with later on. Chaucer puts himself into the story as one of the pilgrims. That, too, is important, but will be the content of a second book: *Pilgrim Chaucer: Center Stage.*

Chaucer actually wrote much more than the *Canterbury Tales*—long poems, short poems, treatises and translations. One of his major efforts was the translation from French of the *Romance of the Rose*. This was the most famous allegory of the Middle Ages. Translating it gave Chaucer the experience of working with allegorical form at its highest level.

The poet was remarkable in many ways. Because he was a commoner, the date of his birth went unrecorded. But his existence became noteworthy for his service to the nobility, as well as several English kings. (One of the kings was Richard II [1377–99], whose life was immortalized in a Shakespeare play.) Chaucer held many official positions, and it's a wonder he found time to write at all. He traveled in Europe often, the first time as part of the English army in France during the Hundred Years War (1337–1475). In his subsequent missions, he would have witnessed evidence of the Black Plague. Outbreaks struck six times between 1348 and 1400. Its virulence, it is estimated, reduced the population of Europe by half between 1300 and 1400. There also would have been opportunities to see some of the great cathedrals being built. A new style we now call *Gothic* was a brilliant departure from the thick walls of dark Romanesque churches. Opaque enclosures dissolved into vibrant jewel-like glass, the structures rising higher and higher, the ornamentation like lace carved in stone.

The Church, in the 1300s, was very powerful, but beset with troubles. It is oversimplified, but still fairly accurate, to say that everyone was Catholic then—happily or unhappily. Chaucer experienced the Great Schism with rival popes—one established in Rome, the other in Avignon (1378–1417). An early heresy was put down by a "crusade" against southern France. The Inquisition continued to pursue heretics on the Continent during and after Chaucer's life. The poet's years held many pitfalls and challenges. He seems to have avoided the pitfalls and triumphed over the challenges.

Here are a few dates that may be familiar and show where Chaucer fits into history:

> Charlemagne was crowned emperor in 800.
> Richard the Lion-Hearted was King of England 1189–99.
> Chaucer lived from about 1340 to 1400.
> The Gutenberg Bible was printed in 1456.
> Caxton printed the first book in English in 1475.
> Luther's ideas became prominent about 1520.
> Henry VIII's break with the Catholic Church came about 1530.
> Shakespeare was at the height of his career around 1600.

With that background in place, I'm ready to tell you about the greatest intellectual adventure of my life. It all began with Geoffrey Chaucer.

Chaucer's Host
Up-So-Doun

Push it. Examine all things intensely and relentlessly. Probe and search each object in a piece of art. Do not leave it, do not course over it, as if it were understood, but instead follow it down until you see it in the mystery of its own specificity and strength.

—Annie Dillard, *The Writing Life (1989)*

I: The Problem

MY PROBLEM WITH Chaucer began not with Chaucer—he was entertaining, stimulating. No, my problem began when I started to read critiques, analyses of the role of the Host, the guide of the pilgrims. The impression the poetry gave me was often the *opposite* of critical opinions. Then I discovered, quite by accident, a fifteenth-century "ally," whose mental image of the Host was similar to my own. This is how it came about.

In accepting the challenge of the word game Chaucer's poetry proposed, I needed to consider all the possibilities in order to progress, to enhance my position. So, while trying to make headway with the *Tale of Melibee*, it seemed like a good move to check the medieval connotations of *prudence*—Prudence being the name of Melibee's wife in the tale. As I scanned the page of the *Oxford English Dictionary* looking for *prudence*, my eye wandered over to the interesting but obsolete *prudenciall*.[1] (I am often attracted to interesting words.) *Prudenciall* was a word I'd never met before, so I paused to make its acquaintance. It handed me an unexpected gift: midway in the entry there was a quote from *The Tale of Beryn*,[2] a poem I'd known about but never developed an interest in, because even though it was once credited to Chaucer, it has been proven spurious. This chance meeting, however, taught me that even spurious offspring of a great writer can have value.

The value here is that a character called the host of Southwark, a deliberate imitation of Chaucer's Host of the *Canterbury Tales*, plays a part in the story's introduction. This reemergence of the Host was an exciting surprise, which provided a unique opportunity to see how an author of the Middle Ages viewed the personality of Chaucer's Host. This anonymous writer provides an important comparison to today's thinking.

I must interject a few words to put your mind at ease. As we begin to look at Middle English works, you need not be put off. To facilitate reading, Modern English is used in the text. (Corresponding Middle English, however, may be found in the notes.) Renderings in today's words are my own, unless otherwise indicated. Where the fourteenth-century word can have more than one meaning, these additional possibilities are noted.

We return, now, to the fifteenth-century characterization. Following our look at the host of unknown authorship, we will view some twentieth-century ideas of the same personage. The host, in the prologue to Beryn's tale, functions much as Chaucer's Host in the *General Prologue*, making arrangements and handling problems of the guests.

At the beginning of the Beryn prologue, the pilgrims have just arrived at Canterbury. Our anonymous poet depicts the host of Southwark, ruler of them all, arranging for their supper on the evening of arrival, before the group had made its visit to the cathedral. When they arrive at the church, a few of the pilgrims behave with disrespect toward their surroundings, whereupon the host scolds them saying, "Peace! Go up and make your offering."[3]

Later he takes the opportunity to thank all of them for the stories they had told while traveling, and recommends they spend the evening relaxing, each man as he pleases, but reminds them that they will rise early for the homeward journey. After the day spent in Canterbury, the group assembles for the evening meal. The narrator sets the scene, commenting that the host did everything prudently as a sober and wise man. "Now let's go to supper," said the host courteously. Following the supper there is an incident with pilgrims doing some late-night carousing while the host is at his accounts; he becomes a bit angry. He asks them politely, nevertheless, to wend toward bed; problem resolved.[4]

In the host's final appearance in the Beryn prologue, he recites a lengthy appreciation that the Almighty Sovereign had sent so fair a day for the journey home. A litany follows of reasons for not choosing the first storyteller by lots (drowsiness, hang-over, hunger, dry mouth, etc.). Finally he suggests that someone begin because of gentlemanliness.[5] The pilgrim Merchant is ready to do the host's bidding and explains why:

> As far as I've sailed, ridden and gone
> I've never seen a man, before this very day,
> Who could rule a company as well as our host can,
> His words are so comfortable and come so in season,
> That my mind is overcome and I can't imagine
> Any reason to go contrary to his wishes;
> Therefore I will tell a tale for your consolation.[6]

And after conventional excuses about his inadequacies as a story-teller, he begins the story of Beryn.

In these scenes, I find the host a well-respected figure of authority, who handles situations courteously, who compliments those who perform properly (even the Lord Almighty), and who has a depth of understanding for human frailties. These are the characteristics the fifteenth-century author understood to be those of Chaucer's Host.

In themselves, the conversations and actions of the counterfeit host do not appear *exciting*. But my excitement comes from discovering a confirmation to my feeling about the personality of Chaucer's Host. I had been offended and confused by very different assumptions about the guide of the pilgrims made by modern writers, such as the following:

> His salient characteristic...is impudence...*our* host plays a comic part, almost from the beginning. He bullies the pilgrims into taking him for guide and master of ceremonies; he brooks no opposition; he makes a point of being rude; he is high-handed at every turn. All this is meant to be funny.[7]

This derogatory twentieth-century view makes it nearly impossible to catch a glimpse of the medieval character. Today Chaucer's Host is often seen as a comic, pompous, money-grubbing cheat![8] In considering how to demonstrate the great change in the accepted personality of the Host, there seemed no clearer way to illustrate the difference than to juxtapose the respected host from Beryn's author with the "bully" view of today. Chaucer's Host has become distorted and out of focus. In the pages ahead, we will see that today's comic interpretation disregards much of the potential of Chaucer's words.

It must be granted that there are many ways to view Chaucer's Host and pilgrims. My reading is certainly not intended to replace others. It reveals a second level of meaning as Chaucer's covert intent. The humor-dominated image of the Host does not allow for the entire personality Chaucer created. Another way of expressing my problem with the Host is that when Geoffrey Chaucer created the role, he had a Paul Scofield in mind—a man for all situations—but somehow when the contracts were signed the part went to Jackie Gleason.

Over the centuries, between Chaucer's day and ours, many decisions about the Host were made and perpetuated. Interpreters delineate a flamboyant braggart, and make it difficult to see the respected medieval figure. There is, within the Host, a personality of strength and integrity waiting to be revealed. The task ahead asks the comedians to wait in the wings, so they can watch as we part the curtain just enough to reveal a medieval drama that has been in rehearsal for six hundred years.

*[The Canterbury Tales] must be read with a full savoring of its
sense, but with the expectation that the sense is designed richly
to embody a sentence, an underlying meaning in
accord with Christian truth.*

—*Bernard F. Huppé, A Reading of the Canterbury Tales (1967)*

II: The Proposal

WHEN THE POEM set the word *Host* spinning toward me, my
Catholic background provided the recognition of its radiance. *Host*
is "a modest sphere containing galaxies." In one cosmic expression
of fourteenth-century thought, it is God's greatest gift to mankind;
it is the Father's sacrifice of His Son. And another representation
of *Host* is God Himself—the Second Person of the Trinity within
the Eucharist. The reverberating potential is awesome. G.K.
Chesterton asserts Chaucer's "fundamental belief in the sacramen-
tal and ecclesiastical system of the Middle Ages," and adds, "those
who do not realize that fact simply do not know the system." The
overseeing presence of the medieval Church could be compared to
the air that was breathed. Miri Rubin presents the medieval
Church as a "narrative of sacramentality...the dominant tale [of]
which embraced man, the supernatural, order and hierarchy, sin
and forgiveness; it punctuated life, marriage, birth and death."[9]

It is the dominance of the Church in everyday life that makes
the proposal, of Christ contained in this Host, reasonable. The
most renowned host of the fourteenth century was the *Eucharistic*
Host. The Eucharist, simply put, was "an axis around which worlds
revolved." To the individual person of faith, "from the very nature
of [the eucharist's] sacramental status, it belonged in every area of
life."[10]

The Dogma of Transubstantiation, promulgated in the thirteenth century, states that the bread and wine of the Mass truly become the Body and Blood of Christ. The *Real Presence* of Christ in the Eucharist came to be celebrated in the Feast of Corpus Christi (Body of Christ). The festival grew in importance in the course of the fourteenth century, with more and more splendid festivities incorporating specially composed liturgies, elaborate processions and dramatized presentations.

Entire communities were involved in these celebrations (Chester, York, etc.). Each year "the leading ceremony was a great procession in which the *host* (the consecrated bread of the Mass), escorted by local dignitaries, religious bodies and guilds, was borne through the streets and displayed successively at out-of-door stations." The feast "provided new contexts of meaning for the eucharist in the feast's evolving iconography."[11]

This was Chaucer's day-to-day world. Picture the poet, if you will, as one of the spectators at this grand procession; see his fertile imagination scanning the scene passing before him, and transposing it into the masterpiece we know as the *Canterbury Tales*. The multiple connotations of *host*, the ambiguity the word contains, enriches the poem's possibilities.

I believe that the character in the *Canterbury Tales*, that we know as *the Host*, is the covert personification of this Eucharistic Host, as he leads the pilgrims who—as in the procession described above—are dignitaries, religious, and guild members. (This identity is a heuristic assumption on my part. I believe this assumption can be clearly demonstrated, and as a result, many oddities will take on real meaning.) To identify the guide of pilgrims as Christ Himself would be in complete harmony with the medieval mind-set.

In order to provide a foundation, and confirm Chaucer's plan, a number of questions occurred to me which needed answering:

Why would Chaucer create covert complexities?
How could he accomplish a hidden meaning?
Why hasn't this identity been seen before?
What makes discovery possible?
What are the characteristics of the fourteenth-century image of Christ?

and Does Herry Bailly (Chaucer's name for the Host) fit the Christ-image?

The answers to these questions will prepare us to open the curtain on the long-awaited performance you've been promised.

Chaucer's keeper of the Tabard is referred to sixty-five times as *the Host*, echoing again and again the cosmic ambiguity. Only once is he identified by a personal name, Herry Bailly. If Chaucer had used *Herry* as the usual designation for the Host, the ambiguous quality allowing the Eucharistic identity would have vanished. Instead, in Chaucer's plan, the poem keeps repeating, "the Host...the Host...the Host," and hopes the reader is nudged so persistently that he becomes alerted to the proper associations.

Though the claim that Chaucer's Host is Christ Himself may be surprising, many have come close to perceiving this image. If more than comedy is expected, a pervading aura, a larger-than-life or God-like quality has been found to emanate from the descriptions and actions assigned to the Host by Chaucer. Critics have commonly associated words of strength and power with this figure. The Host has been seen as *incomparable, dynamic, omniscient, magnificent*, a *moving force*. The Scriptural role of *Servant-Master* is identified with him.[12] And lastly, Ralph Baldwin unwittingly delivers a capsule description of the role of Christ as judge, redeemer, and provider of the eschatalogical supper—the heavenly banquet—although the person being described is Chaucer's Host:

> Not only is this autarch to be sole judge...but he is given *carte blanche* to decide the menu and cost of the supper, and, final absolutism, no one can dissent from his judgment, except by penalty.[13]

Christ-like characteristics are perceived in the actions of the Host, but the full potential of the covert identity goes unrecognized.[14]

Angus Fletcher's informative study, *Allegory*, makes a statement about the ability to appreciate William Blake's poems that can be applied to Chaucer's poetry as well:

> Obscurity appears to be a price necessarily paid for the

lack of universal, common doctrinal background. If readers do not share this background with the author, they may still be impressed by the ornaments of the vision, as "mere ornaments," but these will not for such readers have the cosmic reference of true allegorical language.[15]

For the *Canterbury Tales*, inability to understand, to perceive, may also reflect inexperience with the potential of *inventive* allegory crafted by a genius such as Chaucer.

The cultured reader expected to have to search for different levels of meaning in a sophisticated work.... This feeling for allegorization, for double and triple levels of meaning, is one of the features which distinguished the great works of imagination in the Middle Ages from the mediocre.

—W. T. H. Jackson, The Literature of the Middle Ages (1960)

III: Why Would Chaucer Create Covert Complexities?

CHAUCER IS THE greatest writer in the English language before the time of Shakespeare. It is unlikely that anyone would argue with that statement. And, for me, he is the greatest writer of allegory—of necessity. It is necessarily so because all forms of literature, while he was alive, were steeped in allegory, and his English contemporaries took him to be the finest author of his age. A second reason for the necessity is that he had practiced translating examples of great allegory. Practice would have honed the skills for a job that needed doing.

If the word or idea of allegory is unfamiliar, it is not difficult to understand. Allegory, as mentioned earlier, is similar to parable. Each will tell a story which demonstrates a second and deeper meaning. The parable of the sower and the seed—where some seed fell on good ground and flourished; some fell in weeds and was choked by the surroundings; some fell on rocky ground, sprang up, but soon withered because the roots were weak—is ultimately speaking of the development of faith; the seeds are only a visual image of a spiritual process. Both genres tell a surface story which can be understood and enjoyed, while, at a deeper level, a second message is being delivered. Allegory, however, differs from parable in several ways. The form is generally longer and more complex, and it also deliberately "tries to be obscure." The primary level of allegory "makes good enough sense all by itself. But somehow this literal surface suggests a peculiar doubleness of intention."[16]

The allegorical mode permeated medieval literature, whether it was poetry, drama, sermons, or prose. Possibilities of descriptions and situations, the challenge of analysis and understanding were, to the medieval mind, a delightful and worthwhile pastime, the "highest aesthetic pleasure." The most famous and influential allegory of the Middle Ages comes from France, *Romance of the Rose*.[17] Chaucer was inspired to translate the French poem of more than 20,000 lines; his English version is a reduction, but still contains more than 7,000 lines. No doubt he was well rewarded by what he learned from the French poem.

An allegory has "a structure that lends itself to a secondary reading, or rather, one that becomes stronger when given a secondary meaning as well as a primary meaning."[18] The Middle Ages felt that each story of value had a *lying* (that is, *false*) surface which concealed the truth. This truth is the *sentence*. *Sentence* is a confusing term with a simple definition. The sentence is the hidden meaning, the underlying message.

Lofty or beautiful stories were not the only ones to conceal a second meaning. Amusing stories could also contain a valuable truth. Chaucer's friend, Thomas Usk, faulted the audience (readers/listeners) that might be so distracted by the "deliciousness and jests of a rhyme" that they took little or no heed of the *sentence*.[19] Sentence was the *fruit*—the important element—among the *chaff*. It was the plum to be found hidden among the dense foliage of the story, even a funny story.

The purpose of concealing the most valuable content of a work is not meant simply to try the patience of the reader, though it may seem to be. Boccaccio (d. 1375), the master storyteller, whose works Chaucer knew well, gives a proper explanation.

> Surely no one can believe that poets invidiously veil the truth with fiction, either to deprive the reader of the hidden sense, or to appear the more clever; but rather to make truths which would otherwise cheapen by exposure the object of strong intellectual effort and various interpretation, that in the ultimate discovery they shall be the more precious.[20]

Complexity of the hidden meaning is not only important, it is essential. Knowledge of truth was regarded as precious, a treasure to be gained. Discovery of hidden truth was a prize to be celebrated.

Honor paid to Chaucer by men who knew him (or read his works, not long after his death) has always indicated to me that he was the *best* of allegorists. They drew attention to his "fruitful sentence right delicious" and said "he was expert in eloquent terms subtle and *covert*."[21] This is only proper. The greatest fourteenth-century writer in England should have a reputation that finds his underlying meaning subtle and *covert*. His good friend Thomas Usk, once again, said that in *sentence* no other author surpassed Chaucer.

A twentieth-century writer has said that "we may suspect that in neglecting Chaucer's 'sentence' we are neglecting something which was highly valued by his contemporary audience."[22] It's a point to take seriously. Chaucer's reputation was built by the fourteenth-century audience who greatly admired his works—he was a true "crowd pleaser." This reputation means, to me, that he pleased his audience by constructing brilliant allegories, perhaps more brilliant than some of them realized, and, in my opinion, allegories never to be surpassed.

And, if the Host is the covert image of Christ, as has been proposed, we can suspect that the underlying message will be one of moral inspiration. To see Chaucer as a man of faith, however, need not label him as a religious fanatic. An underlying meaning does not negate or diminish the value of situations and characters we already know and love. (Would we give up reading *Gulliver's Travels* for fun, just because we'd been told a hidden meaning speaks of politics?) From another point of view, those who have wondered how Chaucer could ignore distressing conditions may wonder no longer—may even find greater respect for Chaucer.

Fourteenth-century England was no Utopia, as Chaucer himself recommended to a friend—be not thrall to the world, "Here is not home, here is nothing but wilderness."[23] What a dark thought for a poet some say gave us only humor. We need a truer and more complete picture of Chaucer and the conditions surrounding him, to gain a truer and more complete understanding of what his poetry contains.

I have never been able to imagine an unseeing or unfeeling Chaucer. He had witnessed too many upheavals abroad as well as in England. What moral issue would he address? What would force a reaction from Chaucer? Let's make a quick pass through the fourteenth-century Europe Chaucer had seen.

All of the Continent was overwhelmed by repeated attacks of the plague. Regions of France, devastated by plague and war, gave rise to workers' revolts which were put down by "sweeping massacres of peasants."[24]

Another sweeping attack was that of the Inquisition, which fought the flames of heresy with fire. And within the Church another struggle was raging. In 1378 the reigning pope left Avignon (the seat of the papacy since the early 1300s) and moved to Rome. This newly elected pope, Urban VI, fell into disfavor almost immediately, and a second "pope" (called an *anti-pope*), Clement VII, was elected in Avignon. Evidence and claims from each, as well as counter-evidence and counter-claims, would tax a layman's ability to comprehend it all. Perhaps the hierarchy, too, suffered from confusion. What would resolve the dilemma? This *Great Schism*, as it was called, no doubt added substance to the belief of many that the time of the Anti-Christ, and the end of the world, was at hand as the year 1400 approached.

It's important to understand that "medieval Christianity was merely a synonym for the descending-theocratic form of government, it reached deep into the texture of public life and affected virtually [all] of it." And, because of the theocratic basis, to differ with God's chosen authorities was equated with "high treason." Reconstruction of the judicial system across medieval Europe inclined toward "torture and the inquisitorial process...[as] the prominent characteristic of...criminal jurisprudence." Those who publicly—and even privately—raised objection to the system would have felt "the long arm of inquisitors." "Secret police," a term we all understand, has been used to describe Inquisition technique.[25]

Surprisingly, Fletcher gives an example of just such a situation, where "extreme" censorship is a regimen of "authoritarian government, either secular or sacred." Allegory appears to "thrive" on censorship, as when it "serves political and social purposes by the very fact that a reigning authority (as in a police state) does not see the secondary meaning."[26] By such an analysis, the rigid authoritarian environment of fourteenth-century Europe would have been fertile ground for hidden protests.

Methods of this medieval system touched a particular Englishman in 1385. Cardinal Adam Aston, an English clergyman, was one of six Cardinals in Rome who were accused of conspiracy. (Once accused, it was almost unheard of to be found innocent.) All were seized and confined in an abandoned cistern. They were "subjected to hunger, cold, and vermin...and they were tortured." Because of the "vigorous intercession" of Richard II, Cardinal Aston was released. The fate of the remaining five clergymen is unknown.[27] Could Chaucer have been unaware of this calamity? Unlikely.

The poet had spent his life among figures of nobility. His travels in Europe began as a youth in military service. He had the misfortune of being captured, but was eventually ransomed. Over a number of years, assignments from the king took him all over Europe, at times on missions of utmost secrecy. France—with its wars, peasant massacres, and Inquisition—was territory he covered. Chaucer was on confidential assignment to Italy during the year the papacy returned to Rome. The resulting schism remained unresolved while Chaucer lived.

Conditions prevalent on the Continent could be found on his native soil, as well. His succession of official positions brought him close to many events and aware of their outcome. England was fraught with difficulties, terrors, and disasters. Each siege of the plague—five during Chaucer's lifetime—might last as long as two years.[28] Hardest hit were the peasants and farmers; the dwindling number of able-bodied workers created many complex repercussions. England experienced a Peasant Revolt later than that in France. It was 1381 when a mass of common folk marched on London. King Richard II agreed to concessions, but never found it necessary to live up to them. Necessity vanished suddenly and decisively when the Mayor of London struck the peasant leader dead as the man presented his case to the king.

There were the inevitable political problems of kings with their lords, lords with each other, and lords with a king's successor. One needed diplomatic agility to maintain footing on the political teeter-totter. Chaucer's peace and prosperity was, of course, dependent upon his relationship with the royal court. When his position suffered a reversal, he was removed from the Customs House position he'd held for some time. Taking up residence in Kent, he sojourned outside the royal circle for a time.

Though disaster struck many of those near him, Chaucer (and his works) remained unscathed. Usk, for example (who was quoted earlier, and has been called a *disciple* of Chaucer), was both hanged and beheaded in 1385. Several other friends of the poet who were supporters of Richard II "were executed with varying degrees of shame and severity" by the so-called Merciless Parliament. Dreadful evidence of the crown's justice was brought home to Chaucer when he lived at Aldgate. As a city gate, it constituted "a sort of museum of the heads, arms and legs of traitors, set up there on iron spikes after execution."[29]

An additional threat to Chaucer's personal safety was the heretical Lollard movement (a group bent on religious reform), in which some feel the poet participated. Although the Church took a hostile stance toward Lollard beliefs and activities, the movement attracted followers from many levels of society—merchants, townspeople, clerics, and lords—including four famous knights who were friends of Chaucer. But by 1399 these prominent Lollards "had been...reduced to silence by royal and ecclesiastical pressure."[30]

This pressure also crushed the "intellectual life of Oxford." Books judged harmful were ordered gathered up. (The Church already had a history of book burning.)[31] So a writer who offended authority risked not only personal reprisals, but removal (and perhaps destruction) of his writings as well. If Chaucer considered his message important, he would need to calculate the effect of his words and his actions so that his works would be preserved. Reaching an extended audience would be dependent upon a reputation that did not offend.

Self-preservation could be a daring exploit. "Inquisitors were nowhere and everywhere, roaming about the countryside." When the Inquisition reached England it became even more of a challenge. Religious dissenters were treated with increasing severity. Secular governments were charged with "a legal duty...to exterminate heretics within their domains."[32] Consequently, just a few months after Chaucer's death, the first English heretic to be "found guilty" (William Sawtre) was burned at the stake. Miri Rubin speaks of John Badby (1410) and William White (1428), as well, who both died in the flames. Badby's and White's downfall was their unorthodox ideas involving the Eucharist.

Some time earlier, John Wyclif's career ended with the publication of his protests over the Eucharist. He had been severely critical of faults within the Church, and had encouraged the production of an English translation of the Bible, without Church approval. Ultimately, however, he lost his position and his patron (John of Gaunt) upon publication of his denial of dogma on the Eucharist. I make this connection with the Eucharist to emphasize the importance of the sacrament, once again.[33] Though Wyclif died a natural death in 1384, his bones were disinterred and burned in 1428 as a kind of retroactive retribution.[34] While Wyclif is often seen as a proto-Protestant, it would be one-hundred-thirty-five years after his death before Protestantism was manifested.

The foregoing paragraphs demonstrate that background to Chaucer's writing was not some sort of Merry England; it's time to give the poet a more relevant backdrop—one with a predominance of darker colors. The truth of the situation is "that the Christians of the Middle Ages were unceasingly being called to judgment, often with a suddenness that modern man—for all his *Angst* over the Bomb—can scarcely appreciate." John Lydgate, who knew our poet, took a cue from "his Master Chaucer" by portraying this world as "a thoroughfare of woe" and life as a pilgrimage "in which there is no steadfast abiding (no stability)."[35]

We have looked into *why* Chaucer would have wanted to incorporate a hidden meaning. Many problems could inspire a need to react, let off steam in a quiet, covert way. But why would he persist? Why risk sending a message that could result in death by fearful means? The answer is that it was a matter of conscience. A responsible Christian, who had important information, *must* impart it to others.

Gower (who lived on into the 1400s), for example, writes of moral responsibility to share with others what is received from God. This refers not only to material goods but to insight, to knowledge. Alan de Lille (a great twelfth-century French philosopher) warned that possession of knowledge makes it a duty to impart it—one sinned "who shutteth knowledge in his mouth."[36] There is a sense of urgency here. One must tell others what he understood—God would hold him accountable.

Did our poet feel this sense of urgency? It has been said that Chaucer was simply "amused by abuses" he saw around him.[37] I can not agree with this opinion, because there is much evidence in Chaucer's own words of the great understanding he had of human nature and vulnerability. He had knowledge, there is no doubt, that came from his travels and his closeness to the crown. How could he safely confide knowledge that held the potential of personal jeopardy? He could use the skills, such as allegory, that were his. I believe he was distressed by the possibility of temporal retaliation—but profoundly moved by a certainty of eternal reparation. This world and its problems, however great, are fleeting; the hereafter, unending.

A problem we have, I think, is that we have a tendency to see historical figures (such as Chaucer) somehow suspended in the milieu of their time—but not actually present in the events, not really participating in them. Do we wonder: Did Chaucer ever have a toothache? Did he get caught in the rain and soaked to the skin? Did he have a friend or loved one die in the plague? Did he have an argument with a neighbor—and douse him with wine from his flagon? Did he enjoy dancing? Did he take the same place in church each Sunday to hear Mass? And in 1387 was *Chaucer* one of the crowd in the courtyard at St. Paul's who heard a life-changing sermon—a sermon that six hundred years later is still talked about, and said to be *famous*?

How do we judge the sermon's fame? Is it famous because it was repeated, and parts of it became the nucleus for many other sermons delivered by other preachers?[38] Yes, and Chaucer himself could have heard this sermon that changed many lives.

The preacher spoke at the cross which stands on the grounds next to the famous St. Paul's in London. His words were an apocalyptic message for all Christians, of all stations in life, to review their lives and prepare for the end. Gower and Langland, both late fourteenth-century writers, echo the sentiments of this sermon, and express a similar urgency.[39]

And if this sermon (or a like-minded source) caused Chaucer to want to communicate his personal knowledge—although surrounded by hazards—could conscience exert sufficient pressure for him to follow through? It may be that he lays out his thinking for us to see, to understand in the lines of the *Tale of Melibee* which he reserved for *himself* (Pilgrim Chaucer) in the plan of the collected tales. One of the dictates of Prudence (Melibee's wife) is: "you should always have three things in your heart, that is to say, God, conscience and your good name...you must be careful and very diligent that your good name be always kept from harm." Reiteration of the importance of one's good name continues at length.[40]

Why would Chaucer choose this particular story for his alter ego? It seems likely, in translating *Melibee* from the French, that he found it contained a message he wanted to identify with himself—prudent Chaucer's guiding principle for self-preservation. Prudence, in the story, advises delivering messages discreet and wise.[41] Discreet allegorical messages could be created to please God and soothe the poet's conscience, while at the same time preserving his good name. And, if the poet appeared to be a happy, middle-of-the-road thinker to many of his contemporaries, this was his safeguard. His person and his good name would not be in jeopardy.

To whom were his works, with their message, presented? Initially the royal audience *heard* his words. He was the reciter; he was in control. He could vary accent, raise and lower volume, stress what he wished, create characterizations, even emote, if he chose. The listeners would be influenced by his emphasis. But what of his *readers*—perhaps his most important, surely his most long-lasting, audience? They could read and reread, pause to evaluate, turn back to check a point of interest, and more. The listener hears a performance; the reader, at his leisure, can see, examine, and review the individual words.[42] Depth of knowledge is on the side of the reader.

Chaucer wanted his words to please and he wanted them well cared for. He chose details and allusions from the world around him to delight his sophisticated listening audience. But he was also concerned that his words be copied accurately by his scribe. "He wanted us to *read* him, to open ourselves to the progress of his narratives in ways that are uniquely the privilege of readers, just as he himself had done with [writers before him]."[43] He had read them, studied them. His relationship to each great work was—as Bede recommends—slow, attentive, and laborious. Where his own work was concerned, he wanted each word *he* had chosen to be able to perform for his audience as he had planned.

For two hundred years after his death readers spoke of Chaucer as eloquent, learned, a reformer and teacher of doctrine. He was called "a pure poet, a grave philosopher and sacred theologician." His works were seen "to give profitable counsel…mingled with delight." A respected writer of the sixteenth century even said that he knew of persons who "by reading Chaucer's works…were brought to the true knowledge of religion." The poet's words elicited serious admiration; they seem to hold a communication not obvious to *everyone*. It is as if a group of illuminati were aware of a message so cleverly concealed that it could be overlooked—by the unenlightened, by those not dedicated to pursuing a hidden meaning. Some said that with his words "'in mirth and covertly' [Chaucer] was upholding the ends of true religion."[44]

In the 1500s, when books once again were being examined and condemned, Parliament looked into his works and came "near to deprive us of Chaucer altogether." But there was rejoicing among those who *knew*, when the authorities allowed the poet's works to continue to be read because his writings were adjudged only "jests or toys."[45]

The sixteenth-century's veneration for his poetry seems foreign to us today. How the present prevailing attitude came about will be taken up later. For now, we will close our consideration of *why* Chaucer planned a complex underlying meaning to his tales. The prevalence of allegory, the expectation of a hidden truth, a reaction to distressing conditions, imparting of special knowledge, pleasing of his audience, prodding of conscience, the desire to be found worthy by his God at Judgment—I believe all these things played a part. The world threatened temporal distress; but this was weighed against belief that one's immortal soul faced consequences which were eternal. A concealed Christ could teach many truths to those who would make what Boccaccio called the "strong intellectual effort" to reveal the "precious discovery." When Chaucer and his contemporaries were no more, the truth he had enclosed would live on. He would please God and save his soul.

It has further seemed desirable, if not absolutely necessary...to confine ourselves mainly to the actual texts.

—Geo. Saintsbury, *A History of Criticism and Literary Taste (1900)*

IV: How Could Chaucer Accomplish a Hidden Meaning?

WITHOUT EVEN considering the quality or number of works he produced, the first skill we assume in Chaucer's managing to write is an ability to manage time well. His preparation for the *Canterbury Tales* had come from many years of creativity. He maintained an extensive collection of words drawn from French and Latin, as well as English dialects. He must have loved words—he treated them so nicely, and they served him so well. A large part of *how* Chaucer managed to conceal a meaning—a serious drama behind his comedy—is dependent upon this vocabulary that served him faithfully.

If we look briefly at two poems written by contemporaries of Chaucer, the comparison will give us greater appreciation of the skill of his creations. Both poems are presented as dreams, telling of the sad state of the world. One (*Piers Plowman*) is, in part, concerned with war about church unity. At the end of the poem, the dreamer—who is "Conscience"—in despair, is forced to be a *pilgrim*; the quest is for Truth and genuine authority. In the other poem (*The Assembly of Gods*), "Freewill," who is presented as the servant of "Conscience," must travel *disguised* so as not to be recognized; when questioned and pressed for an important answer, Freewill replies with ambiguity.[46] The two works hold a common message: conscience is portrayed as unsettled, seeking what is true;

open practice of freewill is a risk; ambiguity conceals one's leanings under pressure. With the Great Schism and the spread of the Inquisition, the poems are timely reflections of what may be seen as author reactions to then current conditions.

Comparing these allegories to Chaucer's poetry, at least two observations can be made. One is that the use of conscience, freewill and ambiguity gives us a clue to understanding Chaucer's construction of the hidden meaning in the *Canterbury Tales*: the poet's own personality (as one of the characters) is a *pilgrim on a quest;* and his use of freewill, in speaking out, needed to be cloaked in ambiguities. I don't mean by this that Chaucer was simply imitating, or using the structure of the other poems. What I do mean is that a number of writers were acknowledging distress of conscience, and the peril accompanying freedom of expression. Presentations were one step removed from the real world (as a defense?), as if recalling a dream.

The second observation about these typical allegories is that characters are straightforward abstractions—Conscience and Freewill presented like a labeled pencil sketch. Chaucer, on the other hand, in his atypical constructions, creates a world of living, moving players worthy of today's 3D (three dimensional) images and surround-sound. It took a genius with diverse background, unique imagination, and remarkable courage to give us—to give readers over the centuries—these challenging words which may never be *completely* understood. But what an exciting search for meaning!

Chaucer drew upon his extensive reading in planning the structure of the *Canterbury Tales.* John Lowes, sixty years ago, aptly pictures English, Latin, French, and Italian books over which "Chaucer's mind moved like a magnet."[47] The poet read (and often translated) popular works of his day. Some were translations for his own study, others for adaptation in his writings.

Another area of influence on Chaucer's work is not much talked about. I saw the evidence of it before I understood its source. It's Old English literature. How would Chaucer come upon such an interest? When Chaucer lived, our language had already progressed from Old English to Middle English. The older language and literary styles were obsolete. Old English was as different from Chaucer's English as Chaucer's English is from ours. But the poet himself admits to us through one of his Canterbury pilgrims that "Chaucer" had knowledge of metre and rhyme of the "English…of old time, as knoweth many a man."[48]

Here is the importance of Old English. In trying to get close to the poem, it often seemed as if I were being kept at a distance while the poem leapt about waving a flag. (That's as close as I can come to express what I saw and felt.) In my omnidirectional pursuit of anything and everything that might prove helpful in playing the word game, I looked into translations of early English literature and was taken aback by what John Gardner, in his book on Old English poetry (1975), calls *poetic signaling*.[49] The "flag waving" I had seen was identified. The discovery precisely fit the need.

The *apparent* rebirth of interest in this centuries-old style of verse in the mid-fourteenth century makes it quite clear that Chaucer could have been touched by the early literature. Though it seemed to be a rebirth, it surely sprang from a continuous *oral* tradition. John Lowes describes at some length the opportunities Chaucer had to hear such oral presentations as a boy, a page at court, a customs official on the Thames, and a visitor to the inns of London. Though unrecorded, many very old songs, poems, and stories could have had a lively existence by word of mouth. Then, about 1350, a "magnificent procession of poems" in this old style came forth—*Sir Gawain and the Green Knight* and *Piers Plowman* are examples. They used "much of the old rule" and "something of the old vocabulary."[50]

Though Chaucer's formal development came from Latin and Continental languages, he had a habit of taking "what he thinks fit" from among his many sources. It seems to follow then, that although he put disparaging words about the old-fashioned poems into the mouth of the Parson ("I cannot tell a tale 'rum, ram, ruf,' by letter."), the line serves to demonstrate Chaucer's awareness of this alliterative revival.[51] And as the poet did with other literatures, he could bypass the element that did not interest him (alliteration), and make use of the parts that lent themselves to his purposes.

So, how did John Gardner's analysis of Old English literature help? He outlined "principles governing poetic signaling," which, in my perception, parallel much of Chaucer's style:

1. Poetry tends to allegory.

An image "implies something"; the reader is "teased toward a meaning beyond that which is stated"; the writer "shows what things are somehow significant and what things are not."

2. "Suggestion" is stylistic signaling.

A word, "or in an extended sense, an image, scene, rhetorical flight, etc.,...by its nature stands out from its background...capturing attention...tell[ing] us there is something to be noticed or unlocked."

Repetition "catches the reader's attention and prompts him to ask himself what the point is."

Structural implications are signals when a "seeming mistake of juxtaposition or symmetry, an apparent *non sequitur*" demands our attention.[52]

Signaling, for me, is the main characteristic of Chaucer's poetry. Words *always* seem to be fairly shouting to the reader, "Look at me! Look at me!" Signals are a means "to suggest more than [the poet] says openly."[53]

Donald R. Howard, in his study of pilgrims and pilgrimages, (published in the 1970s) does not use the term *signaling*. Nevertheless, he senses a something-to-be-noticed displaying a signal in his reading of Chaucer's description of the brooch the Prioress (one of the pilgrims) wears. There is "something too complex and too objective to pin down. Such attention to detail is almost sacramental: in such details we conceive a meaning beyond what is evident to the senses." Chaucer's lines, his words, are heavy with meaning, bursting to be understood. Now I recognize what makes me feel this lively burden—the heritage from Old English poetry. This explains why, with his seemingly unlimited vocabulary, he will choose to repeat a word so many times within a few lines (for example, the Host's repetition of *mirth* and *merry* at the end of the *General Prologue*) that the reader becomes fairly irritated by the repetition[54]— as if the poem is pelting us repeatedly with peas from a peashooter, or waving a flag. It does have a purpose; it is signaling to gain our attention.

I indicated, early in this book, that allegory comes in two *very* different types. They are *interpretation*, which is more or less destructive; and *invention*, which is constructive, creative. With the interpretative form, one takes a story from the classics, or a passage of Scripture, and turns and twists it to extract a moral Christian meaning: Ovid's racy *Metamorphosis* turns into messages of *spiritual* transformations; Achilles, Hercules, Orpheus, and others, are said to prefigure Christ.[55] This pressure and distortion has nothing to do with Chaucer.

Walter Ker's capsule summary of the contrasting techniques of allegory explains that,

> when the Middle Ages are blamed for their allegorical tastes it may be well to distinguish between the frequently mechanical allegory which forces a moral out of any object, and the *imaginative* allegory which puts fresh pictures before the mind. The one process starts from a definite story or fact, and then destroys the story to get at something inside; the other makes a story and asks you to accept it and keep it along with its allegorical meaning.[56]

Imaginative allegory is epitomized by the *Romance of the Rose*, the long French work Chaucer translated; it is called "the best known and probably the most successful" in the genre. A strong characteristic of this type of allegory is that it is a "sustained narrative in which all, or almost all, of the characters are personifications of abstract qualities which behave like human beings but are always under the dominant influence of the characteristic they represent," as it would be with Freewill and Conscience.[57]

It was once thought that Chaucer rarely resorted to wordplay.[58] That opinion is no longer tenable. We are discovering that his words know more plays than they've been given credit for.

Part of his plan can be seen from his recruiting the word *ambages* (ambiguity) from the French of his day and adding it to his roster of Middle English gamesters. The medieval intention of the word is not merely ambiguity, but *intentional* ambiguity. Chaucer calls such terms "sly double words that are said to have two faces." Regarding this two-faced doubleness, the poet offers a timeless challenge in his version of the *Romance of the Rose*: "Men may find, whoever has the ingenuity, the double sentence for to see," which sounds as if it is directed to an audience of diligent readers. Kolve recognizes "a long section [in Chaucer's *House of Fame*] remarkable not for any particular poetic eloquence or power...but for the *ambiguity* with which it registers the mode of experience being described."[59]

Even when doubleness waited on the sidelines for centuries, it was found that the poet's apparently "pointless" lines (in his *Book of the Duchess*) were actually not. The words just seemed to ramble: "a long castle with white walls, by St. John! on a rich hill." Then, one hundred years ago, a Bishop of Oxford recognized allusions to Lancaster, Blanche, John of Gaunt, and a reference to John's being the Earl of Richmond—all historical names important in four-teenth-century England. Upon learning about the Bishop's discoveries, a Chaucer expert humbly replied, "It is easy—when you know it.... I certainly ought not to have missed this...we now see a reason for introducing the above lines, which have hitherto seemed rather pointless."[60] Although all the names concealed have to do with Chaucer's personal life, the solution remained unpublished for five hundred years. Perhaps Chaucer planned it so that those who did understand the hidden references would feel a special sense of accomplishment; they would know that they had "the ingenuity" (recorded in his challenge) to discover the double *sentence*.

A further example of word-play—this an imaginative working and reworking of an idea—is explained by Chaucer himself. In the Prologue to *The Second Nun's Tale*, he wishes to expound upon the name of Saint Cecelia. Then, adapting the introduction for St. Cecelia's day (Nov. 22) in *The Golden Legend*,[61] for thirty-two lines the poet takes the name apart and turns it about—associates locations, activities, conditions, effects, and more. His lines demonstrate what can be brought to light from a simple name, and how his poetry can expand and enhance his source. Why insert this lengthy passage of mental ruminations? One reason, surely, is that it was a game the medieval mind enjoyed playing. And it may illustrate the thought process *we* need to utilize in order to understand his mode of working, his nested images.

Chaucer is creative, lively, imaginative in his allegory. Inventions present two meanings which develop simultaneously through the significance of scenes and figures—"as they go along they are usually saying one thing in order to mean something beyond that one thing."[62] (This genre is exemplified by Boethius' *The Consolation of Philosophy*, another of Chaucer's translations.) The outstanding difference between the *Canterbury Tales* and all other such literary creations, however, is the *life* Chaucer breathes into his words, into his characters, rather than allowing them to remain flat, abstract.

His ambiguous words are faithful to his bidding. The most valued of the two-faced words look one way toward the material (tangible), and the other way toward the spiritual (intangible).[63] So, if the poetry offers a word that encompasses both a material and a spiritual sense, it needs to be handled with the utmost respect, because it has a very special job to do. These special ambiguities are often the main problem in trying to animate Chaucer's Middle English with modern words—the tendency is to destroy, to waste part of his meaning. One example will suffice. A recent translation of the *Canterbury Tales* has been hailed as "the best we have ever had,"[64] and yet the last line in this version of the Cook's description in the *General Prologue* will make my point. The Cook, the line says, makes "chicken pudding." This fills the place reserved for Chaucer's "blankmanger." Pudding, in one sense, is an adequate translation. But what has happened to the *white (blanc) manger*? The pale, delicate traceries of a curious alternate meaning are submerged in a dish of pudding. If *blankmanger* is ejected, not allowed it to stay in the game, how will we ever know what secret is hidden in the white manger?

As we consider the poetry's ability to perform, I will interject that the grand adventure with Chaucer is to allow his words to speak for themselves. Excitement is diminished when a "guidebook" prepares us for what we will see. We cannot decide *ahead of time* what a passage will mean. If our mind is filled with an interpretation before we read a tale, it dulls our capacity to have images develop freely, to watch the words in action. When we are programmed for what to expect to see, our goal will be simply to identify what we "know" we should find. Images the words might have produced on first encounter evaporate. Piquancy is lost. Chaucer's meticulously prepared refreshment becomes drab left-overs.

I cannot say often enough how very important *Chaucer's words* are. It could be a serious infraction of the rules the words play by to change, delete, or enhance the content of his lines. Even his *blanks*, the things he avoids saying, are factors, because he chose *not* to clarify, not to disclose more. An instance of this comes in the description of the *Wife of Bath*. We are told that she was without company in her youth. Chaucer follows this disclosure with, "But thereof need not be spoken for now." Why introduce a subject only to express a refusal to enlarge upon it? In 1964, Wolfgang Clemen spoke of these gaps, or purposeful omissions as "a new art of silence, of reserve, of cautious suggestion, unique in his own age."[65] The "uniqueness" is timed, planned, invented; the content of his lines say only what is necessary. The reader needs to be attuned, attentive to the tacit possibilities, the provocative voids.

Another of Chaucer's idiosyncrasies is the tendency to refrain from specifics. In this case, it is not an out and out refusal, but merely a statement with none of the elaboration one expects, as in the providing of a meal with *no* details of what was on the menu. We can't allow this lack to frustrate us to the point of elaborating, or specifying "for the good of the story." And we cannot assume that refraining from giving information has no value, no meaning. Ruskin, for example, takes note of the fact that when Chaucer speaks of the sea—and in his travels he surely had a great deal of experience of the open water—the poet "does not let fall a single word descriptive of the sea."[66] How strange, so much knowledge and yet no inclination to use it.

Another author observes a quality that might easily be overlooked: "in spite of his vividness and lack of abstraction, Chaucer seldom tries to describe an actual landscape or natural scene, or even to give us enough detail to enable us to compose one with any distinctness. It does not seem important to him to do so."[67] What if it is not *lack* of importance, but the opposite which is true? What if the poet declines to describe a natural landscape in detail because it is important for him *not* to do so, *not* to introduce particulars, limitations?

A fascinating conclusion about lack of specifics in the landscapes is that we are not tied to a precise area; we are not influenced in our thoughts by terrain, road conditions, caprices of weather. We are moving in an ideal, detached setting where only Chaucer knows the "landmarks." The reader does not have a clear view to play this game on two levels unless the surface of the story remains uncluttered; the poet cannot fill the surface with concrete objects—trees, houses, church towers. Descriptions must allow an unobstructed field of vision so that we can visualize the ambiguous potential. Little or nothing is said about food, clothing, furniture, or names; when the poet indicates a thing precisely, I have always found it to be significant. Only when physical or otherwise distinct entities compare to the idea in his mind does he put them into play. The meaning of the reticence is that Chaucer has a reason for neglecting to give details.

Another consideration is the unwitting infringement of the rules when words are added for "clarity." The problem with additions to his lines or his images is that added words could alter his intention; they may not be able to play the position; they could destroy a carefully constructed ambiguity (as the "pudding" did). I'll mention only one instance here because it involves the Host directly; we will take it up again in Chapter VIII. When the Host gives his attention to reckonings at the Tabard, he is often seen as money-hungry.[68] The difficulty with this thought is that Chaucer makes no reference here to money. But once actual coins (such as a "grote") are added to the picture, the ambiguous atmosphere is forfeited. The scene becomes shallow, one-dimensional.

For those who would insist on the benefit of clarification, Fletcher cautions the reader to "never lightly assume that clarity is the unclouded aim of most allegory. The mode seems to aim at both clarity and obscurity together, each effect depending upon the other."[69]

Let's also spend a few moments with the artist in Chaucer's words, the source of the pictures before our eyes as we read. (His complex pictures were the beginning of my fascination.) Such images are meant to communicate while they entertain. We see the outlines in our mind's eye; the pictures grow, change, are replaced, or gradually superimpose upon others. We need awareness of what happens with these images because they may be informing us of ideas—as mummers can—without the use of words. The scene where the pilgrims unhesitatingly accept the Host as their judge and guide illustrates this artistry.[70] Interpretation is not verbal. We will examine this scene in greater depth when we scrutinize the Host.

Pictures we see often become so lively that they are more like little dramas. Preparation for the anticipated flood in *The Miller's Tale* has been called an "iconic action," rather like a church window (or a fresco) portraying Noah's flood, come to life. Another example occurs as the Host wakens the pilgrims to set out on their journey to Canterbury. He gathers them in *a flock*, it says, and our mind's eye, for a moment, sees the image of the Host as their *shepherd*, though the word is not used. Kolve demonstrates how the medieval dramatists base action on a "traditional epithet," such as "prince of peace" or "healer of men."[71] We can see the same method here as Chaucer's words conjure a portrait of a shepherd and his flock. These pictures and little dramatizations cause echoes of thoughts not found in the words, registering only in our minds. Being conscious of this strategy will gain a fuller experience of the poetry.

Chaucer is also expert at choosing material. Modifications he makes to his sources need careful evaluation. It has been said that with many of the writings he borrowed, he made "only insignificant" changes. It was common practice to take a known story and translate it, alter it, expand it, or even combine two or more stories. It was the way the Middle Ages (before the printing press) kept good material circulating. Plagiarism was never associated with the practice. We would be inclined to ask about the changes; why alter borrowed material if the change is going to prove insignificant, meaningless? It would be simpler not to make the change. But perhaps there is a purpose not yet discovered. I am inclined to agree with the differing opinion that "every addition or omission that [Chaucer] makes is worthy of careful attention."[72] The changes, large or small, can tell us something about the poet's thought process, perhaps even something about his intention. We are fortunate to have the means to make comparisons.

For such comparisons, I like to picture Chaucer working in the way Annie Dillard describes for the poetic process, his product growing by minute, breathtaking operations—each line tapped into place by a jeweler's hammer.[73] I see him select an old piece and begin to turn it over slowly, carefully, to discover the most effective view. Rough edges are smoothed. Weak connections are strengthened or replaced. He discards an ordinary stone, inserts a precious gem in its place, and I appreciate the effect of the exchange. A last bit of polish adds a glow that hadn't been seen in its previous condition. He has made the work his own; he has skillfully brought to the surface all he had seen of the potential as latent promise.

Of course his intimate relationship with the words he employed deserves attention. Though we may be led up a fool's path by his poem (due to our limited knowledge of fourteenth-century connotations), we cannot assume any limitation on his part. A common meaning today (such as our familiarity with *buxom*) may not function as he intended at all. And it is obviously true that Chaucer did not know the order of dictionary entries that would result today. Any of the definitions, from *1a* to *6c* and beyond, is possible as his intention—if it is of proper age, will do the work required, and is on good terms with its neighbors.

A dedicated reader needs adequate tools so that meanings common to Chaucer that have become submerged may be helped to resurface. Our poet's vocabulary celebrates our language; preparation is needed to be able to participate in the celebration. Although Richard Altick is speaking of the background necessary for reading Shakespeare, his words ring true for Chaucer-lovers as well:

> We need a thorough acquaintance with [fourteenth-century] medicine, religion, costume, superstition, crafts, political theory, ornithology, music, law, sport, table manners, military and naval practices, and scores of other topics.[74]

It is the job of the audience to fill in details, to know how to relate statements made in the poem; preparation to do the job adequately demands knowledge. It is probably not difficult to agree that if a rendering into Modern English tends to remove double-entendre from Shakespeare, we do the playwright a disservice; part of the life of his words has been stifled. We need to feel the same concern for the medieval vocabulary. If we want to play the game fairly, treat his words with true sportsmanship, we cannot make unwarranted or unfair substitutions. If we eject what are agile but unrecognized line-backers, leave them idle, how can the poem give its all?

Several of his words resonate naturally. They sound again and again, sight unseen. *Pilgrimage*, for example, is part of every line— it expresses the purpose of the travelers and the progress toward Canterbury. Though intensity of response to the word may have diminished since the fourteenth century, it hasn't disappeared. A sense remains that we are pilgrims in this world, and daily life our pilgrimage. Medieval man was reminded each day that he was on a journey to meet his Maker. Residue of such knowledge continues to be perceptible in the word. An automatic reaction is perceived regarding *Pilgrimage;* an automatic reaction is stimulated by *Crusade* and *Inquisition*—they are more than words. We *feel* them.

Judgment (Middle English, *doom*) is another sensation that recurs throughout the *Tales*.[75] It is the reason the stories are told. It touches each pilgrim and each story—mentioned or not. *Host* too influences the entire work. The word is a part of every action. Each character has his or her eyes and ears directed toward the *Host*. The vibrating resonance of the name *Cecelia*, noted earlier, demonstrates a method of medieval analysis. Chaucer knows how words behave. They are not silent markings on a page; they are alive and participating with each other to catch and hold our attention while they try to deliver the message that has been entrusted to them.

In comparison, Boccaccio, who told us why important messages are concealed, wrote a collection of stories early in the fourteenth century. Boccaccio's *Decameron,* as the collection is called, has been found to be "more audacious and new, [but] it is also less rich, less substantial, less resonant in the mind" than the *Canterbury Tales*.[76] Chaucer's originality gave us a work far greater than the sum of its inspirations.

We have been looking at *how* Chaucer could have hidden a message beneath the surface of his poetry. He had sufficient background and experience with allegories of his predecessors. His unequaled skill with manipulating words and images set him apart as a master of inventive technique.

And, by a fortunate coincidence, there was an actual innkeeper in London whose name was "Henri Bayliff," and an establishment that was called the "Tabard Inn." Some said, with the discovery of this information a number of years ago, that these were the obvious inspirations for Chaucer's character and setting.[77] Another view, however, clearly shows that this reality may have given the poet inspiration for his own personal safety. If an inn and an innkeeper with the same names exist, it would be "understood" by his contemporaries to be the basis of his *Tales*. Nothing more would be suspected. But once again the poet made one of his "insignificant" changes, using *Herry* instead of the real innkeeper's *Henri*—and the Canterbury pilgrims are sheltered in the *Tabard*, which Chaucer *never* refers to as the *Tabard Inn*.

These minimal differences signal the skillful plan for a hidden meaning only revealed to those who make the strong effort to challenge the poem at every line, in order to come to grips with Chaucer's depth and complexity. We are dealing with a clever poet, a loyal Englishman, and a serious Christian.

The nature of fictions has become a major issue of our time and is
likely to remain so, for we habitually address the issue by asking
about the relation of fiction to reality, knowing we are quite a bit
less certain than former ages were that we know what is real....
Chaucer invites us to surmise that this meaning is available to
a detailed examination of objective reality, though after a
century of Chaucer scholarship it turns out it is not.

—Donald Howard, *Writers and Pilgrims (1980)*

V: Why Hasn't This Identity Been Seen Before?

IF WE HAVEN'T seen all that the *Canterbury Tales* can mean, it should not surprise us. We are dealing with a most clever poet from a period little understood. One of his devoted friends said of him that his manner of writing, his use of imagination and reason within the *sentence*, surpassed all other writers.[78] In spite of the minimum of detail that was his style, his fictional situations and conversations come alive.

True appreciation of the liveliness, however, is found in the *fourteenth-century* words. Most readers today are at a disadvantage relating to Chaucer because of the Middle English. It is not that reading his language is impossible, but most will not take the time or cannot work up the confidence to develop a personal relationship with the poems. It's rather like being too inhibited to make friends with a Swedish-speaking family who just moved onto the block. Your life will go along very nicely without becoming acquainted with them; the proof is simple—you've done very well without knowing them up to now. And knowing a Swedish family or reading Chaucer is not a necessity—to most people.

Chaucer's *manuscripts* were just that, *hand-written*. About one hundred years after his death the printing press appeared and some of the manuscripts were set in print. One hundred years after Chaucer's first manuscripts were printed, Shakespeare was writing.

And during Shakespeare's early life Chaucer could still be honored with the title "God of English Poets."[79] But England was changing rapidly. Firm foundations were quaking; a new style of thinking swept old ideas away. The 1500s saw the spiritual break with Rome, the emergence of Anglican, Puritan, and Presbyterian factions. Several translations of the Bible into English became available. Chaucer was one of the old ideas (expressed in old language), and with the change in ideas came a change in his reputation. His audience diminished; his language became an archaic oddity. Efficiency of the printing press gave readers many works easier to enjoy.

As the Middle Ages grew more distant (1500 is the date often arbitrarily used as the end of the Middle Ages), unrecorded knowledge that had been part of the ordinary fabric of daily life disappeared. One example of such loss is knowledge of construction of the great cathedrals. Attaining the brilliant colors of the glass and methods of constructing the vaulted ceilings were secrets of the trades, passed from one craftsman to another. These secrets are gone.[80] Chaucer, too, was once well known, but knowledge to associate with his works has faded. If there were formulas for understanding allegories, they too failed to be preserved.

In attempting to renew the relationship with Chaucer's work, some assumed the task would not be difficult because his phrasing seems "remarkable for its crystalline and limpid simplicity." The same reviewer soon granted that this impression is short lived, and concluded that "Chaucer has the faculty of seeming more simple than he is." His "crystalline simplicity" is an illusion. First impressions can be misleading. It is much more true that "we shall undoubtedly find that Chaucer was an artist whose subtlety, humor, and power fully justified his early reputation."[81] Chaucer's "power" with words is the prime factor preventing easy penetration of the surface, the deterrent in reaching the *underlying sentence.*

Great literature of the Middle Ages enclosed a meaning to challenge and delight its audience. Strong Augustinian influence encouraged a difficult construction so that achievement of the insight gained would be more precious. Truth was hidden in a way that "rendered it quite useless to the multitude," that concealed it "from the unworthy."[82] It seems that most people were never intended to understand the *sentence*, the covert message. We are being challenged by unexcelled poetry to find the proper tools, to discover an appropriate means of parting Chaucer's ornately woven curtain in order to view a new *truth*.

Surely a strong reason for not uncovering an underlying sentence in the *Canterbury Tales* is that the surface story is so distracting, so diverting. The reader is truly diverted, turned aside. Chaucer's creation is so thoroughly pleasing that readers would feel that only an ingrate would ask for more.[83] But there *is* more. After this long, dark sojourn, it deserves to be brought to light.

Our ever-changing language caused a die-hard champion of Chaucer (in 1658) to scold those who were critical of the poet's English: "Blame him not (Ignorants) but your selves, that do / Not at these years your native language know." But it was a lost cause. What little interest remained saw the poet bent on humor, and complained about his coarseness.[84] I wonder if the complaints of coarseness indicate the loss in perceiving deeper alternate intentions in the words, and situations—or a change in what was simply considered less acceptable in humor. The reason behind the complaints is not altogether obvious.

His reputation plummeted until it was rescued late in the seventeenth century by John Dryden, the English author, who described Chaucer as superior to ancient classic writers. This renewed interest, however, actually turned readers away from the original texts; for this new audience, his language was modernized—we've seen what that did to the *white manger*. His carefully chosen words were no longer recognized, treasured. His name was better known, but his real words were not. Readers of the 1800s commonly complained of primitive style and "the most direct and coarse terms."[85]

A true Chaucerian renaissance begun by Victorians exhibited great interest in the works and in the man. With minimum evidence and maximum confidence, they constructed an image of the dead poet. Although there exists only a smattering of recorded entries about Chaucer in legal documents (for example, a court case, a sum of money or other compensation awarded the poet, his change of residence noted, etc.) a wide variety of conclusions were drawn. One writer concluded Chaucer had been an unhappy husband—but a tender, loving father. Another saw the poet living in constant tranquillity. Still another claimed the poet's writing allows knowledge of Chaucer "from soul to skin." A medieval likeness of the poet inspired the statement that this was a portrait of the poet when he was *ill* not *old*. And, the ultimate presumption, he was declared "senile."[86]

Regarding his works, two fundamental statements were made. One was a decision that the poet had *freed* himself from allegory. Kittredge went so far as to say, "Chaucer, they tell us, is very modern. So he is; this crisis [in one of the tales] proves it." Not only was a declaration of modernism made by a noted scholar, but it was backed up with proof. That must have been difficult to refute. Another early reviewer saw his writing naïve because of "the times in which he lived and wrote."[87] The first opinion placed Chaucer outside the fourteenth-century milieu that loved allegory; the second ascribed little value to writings of the Middle Ages, a period which was held as primitive, unenlightened. It is more likely that it was Victorians who were naïve—in relating to the fourteenth century. Scholars of the 1800s had prejudices to overcome, as well as being handicapped by a lack of authoritative information. They made the start, however, and we should bless them for that. But it would be unjust to perpetuate faulty information about Chaucer, if we find such.

One element of mid-nineteenth century England was a zealous concern over Catholic vs. Protestant identification. As G. K. Chesterton puts it, there was a Victorian convention "according to which a literary study should not refer to religion, except when there is an opportunity of a passing sneer." Questions of Chaucer's religious loyalties found him, on the one hand, "hostile…to the church of Rome," and, just as confidently, on the other hand, "remain[ing] what he had been—a good Catholic."[88] It was a time when definitive statements could be made without insisting on evidence we would demand today. (For example, spontaneous combustion of the human body was still accepted as a cause of death.)

Demands of evidence aside, however, the insistence on identifying Chaucer's convictions of faith takes us far afield. What does this have to do with appreciating his poetry? Lines are read differently when viewed through prejudicial opinions, especially if "evidence" is being sought to support a pro- or anti- view. The poetic sense will play a lesser, rather than the all-important part it deserves.

Uneasiness over religious subjects was also a problem in the Chaucer renewal. When confronted by medieval declarations about Chaucer's "zeal" for religion, the concept was written off because "no one is now engaged in circulating his writings with the object of converting men to the true faith."[89] Even though the means for inspiring conversions was not evident to the nineteenth century, it is misleading to act as if it had never existed.

Finally, some looked at the jolly teller of tales with confusion, and were "embarrassed by [Chaucer's] overtly religious" works, *The Parson's Tale*, for example. They tried to deny parts of it a place in the canon.[90] Realize from this that Chaucer's canon had not yet been confirmed—and yet definitive statements were constructing weighty Chaucer criticism on a foundation, by today's standards, of less than necessary depth.

The fundamental rejection of allegory by the Victorians has stunted development of its positive research. We now know, on good authority, that inventive allegory became ever more popular from the thirteenth century on. Its grand variety of personifications (as in *The Romance of the Rose*) behave as human beings: Wicked-Tongue, we hardly need be told, "saith never well." Some of his fellow-players are Reason, Idleness, Jealousy, etc. This method of medieval storytelling, found in all forms of important literature, is neglected now (according to *A Preface to Chaucer*, 1962) because of the persistence of strong prejudice: "Allegory is almost universally regarded with suspicion, if not with contempt," and is adjudged "tedious" and "the province of specialists."[91] These strong feelings are partly due to *interpretive* and *inventive* allegory being so consistently lumped together. Distortions of the former have prevented enjoyment of the latter.

Allegory also eludes scientific detection; modern scholars wish to confine themselves to what a text "actually says." The flaw in this desire (as we saw with the pudding/manger) is that if you deny allegory, you actually *deny* complete content—what the text truly, ultimately says. Authors, using "scientific philology," have tried to gain the advantage over "our plodding medieval ancestors," but by their own admission, this *scientific method* does not do the job.[92] Shrouded imagery and fast-moving stories, like many in the *Canterbury Tales*, can deceive or seduce a reader to neglect an allegorical message. The fascination of the "literal surface then becomes sufficient unto itself."[93] A subtle game is being played: if we only skim the surface of an allegory, we never become involved with the action on the inside. Granted, it is easier—but not as exciting—not to get involved.

The world Chaucer created is not peopled with flat figures like Jealousy or Wicked-Tongue. His pilgrims function on more than one level. With this masterful touch, you hardly notice that they are not *real* people. Their designations are not names, but *functions*—Prioress, Miller, Plowman, Wife, etc. Despite this limitation, you feel, by the end of the *Tales*, that you have become acquainted with a personality for each character. The Host and the Wife of Bath, in particular, captivate audiences. Without doubt, they are two of the greatest characters in all of English literature.

The importance of each pilgrim's *function*, and the importance of *Chaucer's* words, once again, can be inadvertently destroyed if we are not dedicated to preserve what the poet says. Just consider, if we distort the personality of the Host, we distort *the central force*, the director of the action. (It also makes an essential difference—a difference in essence—if a function is redesignated, for example, as when the *Wife* of Bath is called "a business woman"[94] in a recent Modern English version. Her *wifeness* is diminished; part of Chaucer's intention is lost.) Unless *his* words are followed whither they will lead, his words cannot challenge, inform, and delight as his genius intended.

Yet another dilemma exists which keeps us from being on an intimate basis with the writings. Several of Chaucer's creations (mainly prose works) have been confined by the verdict of "dullness"; their confinement will not allow them to gesture, to express themselves. Visitation is reserved to the "sturdy specialist." One such piece is the *Tale of Melibee*, told by Pilgrim Chaucer. Balanced testimony, with an eye toward the fourteenth century as well as the modern audience, informs us that this is "a moral work which had an extraordinary reputation not very easy to understand or appreciate now."[95] I appreciate that statement because it tells of more than the present negative value of *Melibee*; it tells of the story's original importance, as well. It is necessary to know that its medieval reputation was no less than "extraordinary." We need help with perspective so that, with restrictions lifted, the tale can once more be allowed to circulate in society. Someone willing to give the case of *Melibee* a sensitive and thorough review is needed. The job would be easier for a specialist, but someone interested in restricted words might do the job. Dedication and fascination go a long way in the Tale's rehabilitation, reanimation. Who knows what its words might add to our knowledge of Chaucer, if they are once more recommended for action.

Victorianism, once again, formed other opinions we live with today. It was said that "the naughty story" would "require no treatment." What have we missed because of a hands-off (eyes-closed) attitude toward some subjects? Consider the story told by the Pilgrim Cook, who claims his offering is a "little joke." In spite of the claim, this fragment of a story, adjudged "too short to disclose the plot," was declared exceedingly vulgar because of the mention of a prostitute.[96] If we allow, however, that the Cook might really just be telling *a little joke*, this could be an innocent subject hiding behind a risqué exterior—as we find in medieval riddles. Reevaluation needs to begin with a blank page.

Hesitation, in lending the mind to an eyes-forward look at "naughty" situations, finds a parallel in the disinclination to consider tainted language. Scandalous words were denied permission to speak. A perfect example is the story of Sir Thopas, where Chaucer's oft-repeated *pricking* (of a horse) is replaced by "pumping the unhappy steed." *Drastiness*, which caused this tale to be interrupted by the Host, was defined by reviewers as "worthless." While this is accurate, it is not the whole story—the medieval word can also intend "filthy."[97] Since the decision was made for *worthless*, a balanced claim for *filth* is hard to find.

Lack of nineteenth-century willingness to deal with Chaucer's words and situations has pushed complex and ambiguous elements into verbal quarantine. The strength of our contemporary faculties should give us confidence in releasing these stricken individuals. They are not beyond hope. Verbally renewing their license will not influence the rules of the game. We may be able to live quite securely when we see them only as carriers of infectious *humor*.

We are also deprived of a wider appreciation of Chaucer's lines, because almost every aspect of the poet's reputation has been lost—except that of jolly storyteller. Comic interpretations of the Host abound; comic intentions, read into Chaucer's situations, run rampant. Regardless of apparent straightforwardness, we are told that all "is meant to be funny"—the silence of the pilgrims as they approve the Host's plan, the Host's bow to the respected Knight, the story of Melibee (elsewhere considered interminable and dull), the choice of a serious word (implying *verdict*) when a judgment will be made[98]—all these have prompted, what are to me, misdirected assumptions of humor. Such assumed comedy prevents a serious characterization of the Host.

Another handicap, the intrusive thoughts of *money* in lines where it is never mentioned, encourages an image of a Host who tends to his guests "but never forgets his own interests," and whose plan to "make money…is undeniable."[99] Monetary intrusions present a Host whose money pouch is a prominent feature of his appearance; we see it every time he comes into view. But he was not invested in this way by Chaucer.

Alternative plans that attempt to make reality of the adventure can also change our perspective. Chaucer's spare design allows for minimal detail of the way and the means of the journey. This maximum of blank space encourages some to fill in, to change the focal point. There is a proposed plan that achieves a *round trip* that lasts six days, and another that goes only one way, but takes three days for the journey.[100] As reasonable as these proposals may seem, they are not *Chaucer's* plan. In the *General Prologue*, the pilgrims are up at sunrise and the last story is ready to be told when sunset is imminent. Chaucer devises a clear, almost transparent setting. He puts in place only the ambiguous essentials. He presents *time* free of moment-to-moment progress. This meshes with the plan for bare, unidentifiable landscapes. To clutter our minds with practical information obscures the deliberately chosen span. We'll return to the importance of the time element again.

With planned concealments on Chaucer's part, loss of understanding when interest in his writing ebbed, Victorian influences, prejudice against allegory, apparent need to see everything as comic, and see details as *real*, it is no wonder that an underlying meaning has not surfaced. Changes in English over six hundred years discourage most from tackling Chaucer's original words—where the meaning is hidden. And so we often deal with that "comic, pompous, money-grubbing" Host. A great loss.

The *Tales* are a puzzle of tightly designed pieces. Chaucer-lovers can make great advances in this word game through the scholarship brought to light during our century. Using information that was not available to Victorians gives us knowledge needed to form a new image of Chaucer, and of his Host.

The greatest of older poets, Shakespeare as well as Chaucer, became half invisible.... Brilliant reëxamination of the post-Victorian Shakespeare has already taken place. The whole critical atmosphere of today is propitious for rediscovery of poetry lost and poetic meanings inappreciable to older generations.

—Charles Muscatine, *Chaucer and the French Tradition (1957)*

VI: What Makes Discovery Possible?

TWENTIETH-CENTURY research into Chaucer—his work, and his world—has given us authoritative information never dreamed of by early Chaucer scholars. We now see the naïveté of the nineteenth-century approach to the medieval period. Lack of understanding saw high artistic accomplishment as the output of unskilled craftsmen.

Incomparable cathedrals, built in the centuries before, during, and just after Chaucer's period, had been seen as folk-art. Truth about the construction began emerging in the middle of this century:

> It is high time, now [1952], that the facts have begun to be told about the building of the cathedrals. Yet legends persist, and one of the most charming depicts an emotional army of volunteers, each with a stone, all singing strongly, arriving from every direction to deposit rock upon rock as the churches rose in a haphazard surge of common will.[101]

Those in the past, who had considered the creation of these splendid edifices, were blind to the necessary craftsmanship and esthetic plan. Today's builders probe accessible evidence in an attempt to gain a true appreciation of the marvel of organization and strength these centuries-old structures represent.[102]

In addition to an often simplistic attitude, scholars in the nineteenth century were unknowingly hampered by the lack of information and services we take for granted. We can be overwhelmed with the amount of information readily available now, but even sixty years ago adequate source material for medieval studies was scarce, and what has been accomplished by Chaucer scholars in little more than one hundred years is remarkable.

In 1868 the Chaucer Society was founded. Its sole aim was to produce and print proper texts of Chaucer's works. In 1870 the Society had only one hundred members, and a "satisfactory and authoritative text" of the *Canterbury Tales* did not yet exist.[103] Now having authentic editions of all of Chaucer's works at our fingertips is assumed.

While appreciating the texts produced, we must be aware of the philosophy and attitude incorporated into commentaries about Chaucer's writings. We cannot fault the effort—but we must be ready to modify previous assumptions with new and more accurate information. Prejudiced statements (such as those supposedly divulging knowledge of his personal attitudes[104]) must be seen for what they are—only speculations—and not be granted the authority of real evidence regarding Chaucer.

Before modern scholarship existed, the poet's words were often glum, feeling misjudged, misunderstood. They continued with their basic duties, but their sparkle had waned. (They saw up-to-date words trying to take their place.) New aids to scholarship have resuscitated them, given them new hope. They need another chance—let's not disappoint them.

The 1950s were especially important in Chaucer scholarship. The decade was the source of Muscatine's call for reevaluation that heads this chapter.[105] Deep insights, and much general medieval information, have since been published. New knowledge needs to be applied to Chaucer's works as if his poetry were being examined for the first time. This new wealth of resources can be an implementation that may lead to a new direction in thinking.

Outstanding observations came from Ralph Baldwin, who described the "Unity of *The Canterbury Tales*" (1955). His analysis makes reading the *Tales* a new experience. Relationships are identified that had gone unrecognized, rather like the discovery of the references in the otherwise "pointless" lines in *The Book of the Duchess*.[106] We cannot regret that such understanding was late in coming; the important thing is that Baldwin's vision gives an exciting new viewpoint. Structure of the *Tales* had generally been seen as an unfinished collection of stories within a frame. "Unity," however, is now detailed. It defines an essential purpose, a unified view of the entire work.

Alongside Baldwin's remarkable feat, Chaucer-devotees rejoiced at the beginning publication of the much-needed *Middle English Dictionary* (subsequently noted as MED), an ongoing enterprise begun in 1954.[107] Chaucer-reading to that date was done without an adequate dictionary of Chaucer's language. Pioneering scholars labored under this handicap with perseverance, dedication, and resourcefulness. Now the University of Michigan at Ann Arbor has become the nucleus of interpreting medieval intent. We can see more clearly the "rules" the words use as they play their game with us. Virtually drawing from works produced only from 1200 to 1500, definitions are specifically applicable to Chaucer and other medieval writers in the English language. Before Ann Arbor took on this momentous task, the OED (*Oxford English Dictionary*, earlier called the NED, *New English Dictionary*), was the faithful servant. Though the OED may seem to have existed "from time immemorial," it was actually published between 1884 and 1928, and still serves where MED fascicles—*u* through *z*—have not yet appeared. One comparison, however, will illustrate the benefit we gain from the Michigan effort as we seek to recognize medieval creativity.

The word *courtesy* in the OED has three possible definitions before 1500 with six quotations to illustrate usage; an entry regarding application to law has one citation, and that is from 1523. The comparable *courteisie*, in the MED, on the other hand, provides five possible definitions with seventy-five quotations; the law entry has three medieval examples of usage. MED examples are not only more numerous, but more diverse and more deeply informative of medieval connotations and applications. Words that we've seen in a straightforward presentation may now reveal to us that they are capable of wearing masks at times, taken to be silly when their situation has a possible serious tone as well; or we may find one word has a "double"—an actual Gemini. With this new dictionary, Chaucer's audience will find the sets in the drama of the *Canterbury Tales* more detailed and his stage-lighting improved.

Though the 1950s were especially important, there actually has been a general growing interest in things Chaucerian from the turn of the century. Ancillary works have provided clearer associations for the Chaucer canon and its related history. One such work gives us historical literary perspective. Caroline Spurgeon collected *all* the written entries, from his lifetime forward, that mention Chaucer or his writings. Her work, *Five Hundred Years of Chaucer Criticism and Allusion* 1357-1900, was published in book form in the early 1920s.[108] Scholarly privilege to search through archival materials is no longer needed. Authoritative information, the catalog of ebb and flow of interest, as well as shifts in the bases of opinions regarding Chaucer is now in libraries everywhere. Spurgeon reflects that the "criticism Chaucer has received throughout these five centuries in reality forms a measurement of judgment—not of him—but of his critics."[109] This century will surely be judged by how we have used our wealth of available information.

Add to this new historic information a complete alphabetic index of Chaucer's vocabulary and usage. In 1927 *A Concordance to the Complete Works of Geoffrey Chaucer* was published.[110] Ideas can be checked confidently and thoroughly, for their affirmation or rejection, with very little effort. The poet's statements about Christ, for example, have been very important to this project. What direct statements did Chaucer make regarding doctrine? What physical descriptions of Jesus are there, if any? This essential word-list makes the quest a simple, rather than an arduous, task.

While we are checking Chaucer's words, we may want to compare them to his source. Some important side-by-side comparison for the *Canterbury Tales* has been facilitated. A number of the tales are direct translations, others bear only a resemblance to earlier stories. The modern reader, using *Sources and Analogues of Chaucer's Canterbury Tales* (1941)[111] can pinpoint where Chaucer made his "insignificant" changes, what was added, what deleted. What do these differences mean to us now, now that we have all this new information to aid our thought processes? If Chaucer changed a character's name, did it become more meaningful? Meaningful in what way? If he changed the intensity of a description, or deleted a description, how does that alter the meaning of the story? This one volume provides the material for extensive consideration and discernment.

Angus Fletcher's stimulating analysis of allegory as a symbolic mode, which has already been of assistance, is essential reading for understanding Chaucer's technique. And a very recent addition to our knowledge of things medieval, Miri Rubin's *Corpus Christi*, is a thorough study of the historical, political, theological, and sociological developments surrounding the Sacrament of the Altar, which was "the centre of the whole religious system of the later Middle Ages."[112]

Publications named above are just a few that provide easy access to authoritative texts, perceptive analyses, definitions and connotations, historical information and important sources. With all these aids on the shelves of any fine library, Chaucer-lovers have more time for reflection, comparisons, and speculation. What once was a luxury (for privileged, much-traveled specialists) can now be the pastime for any devotee with a medieval passion.

I have found great inspiration in another readily available book, Richard Altick's *The Art of Literary Research* (1963). It gives the reader with a strong sense of curiosity the courage to think about "fundamentals" that seem out-dated, or irrelevant. Altick says we must not hesitate to question "a speculation that has been dignified into a 'certainty'; ...an assumption of critics or literary historians which has gone unchallenged so long that it now seems as impregnable as an old-fashioned Gospel truth."[113] Such questioning could revitalize Chaucer ideas that have *petrified*. The "Marriage Group" (coined in 1908, popularized in 1912) for example, has been the standard way of classifying several of the stories.[114] Though the *Group* seems a fixture, it was not so named or categorized by Chaucer. The will to reevaluate might help us see a plan much more imaginative, much less mundane.

Before we are led to theorize, however, we need solid information about the Middle Ages. To our great good fortune and considerable delight, many scholars have produced very readable books to be enjoyed as we gather background about the world of Chaucer's day.

Gerald Owst has provided us with a thorough, and thoroughly entertaining, study of fourteenth-century sermons, contained in two books published in 1926 and 1933, originally. He doesn't hesitate to take modern writers to task who express opinions and theories about other medieval literature while failing to consider the influence of sermons. Doomsday, he explains, had long been a popular topic of the Middle Ages. It would often be presented in a dialogue, with Christ as Judge hearing witnesses from heaven and hell, to determine the fate of a particular sinner. Owst gives examples of many preaching techniques—satire, allegory, humor, and various types of imaginary dialogues, as well as scenes of Judgment Day—all of which influenced medieval writers. And he challenges: "Did Chaucer himself, indeed, never sit with laughter-loving 'wives of Bath' who went regularly 'to preaching' because it amused them, and join in the uproarious merriment that greeted the preachers' witty caricatures in London, that city of many pulpits? The poet's own merry laughter seems to rise up before us from the page and mock his would-be interpreter."[115]

Owst also speaks of the famous sermon at St. Paul's Cross mentioned earlier. Though this sermon ("the most famous sermon ever delivered at Paul's Cross") was commonly referred to, and quoted from for many years, the entire text was not available to the interested reader until 1967.[116] Before that, only the actual historic texts existed.

This sermon of influential exhortation—"Yield reckoning of thy bailly"—telling of the Day of Judgment which was fast approaching, had been composed and preached by Thomas Wimbledone. He told his listeners that "the great Antichrist should come in the fourteen hundredth year from the birth of Christ, which number of years is now fulfilled with not quite twelve and one half years lacking." Many preachers were moved enough by Wimbledone's message to use parts of it in their own sermons. How much of an effect, we need to ask, did it have on the laity, on the listeners who would spread it directly to others? What if Chaucer himself had been at St. Paul's Cross to hear it? Wimbledone, reviewing prophetic signs, asked, "Who doubts that the world is at the end?" Priests, knights, and all other Christians were called to prepare, "then shall Christ ask reckoning."[117]

Chaucer could have heard Wimbledone exhort that if you don't care about your own welfare, or dying suddenly without being forgiven for serious sins, at least think of desiring great joy and fearing great pain. The preacher concluded: "He is nigh."[118] These sobering thoughts might evoke sufficient penitence to inspire a serious examination of conscience, and perhaps a conversion of heart.

As more information about the Middle Ages becomes available, we are also learning how much there is yet to discover. One author (in 1961) recommends that conclusions are difficult because "much more needs to be known about the intellectual life of four-teenth-century England than is possible at present. Too much important material lies buried in Latin manuscripts not well known or not easily available for study." Another author (in 1978), interested in fourteenth-century religious thought, contends "We have only just begun to discover and analyze the sources and resources of this world of thought, so that an assessment at this point is perforce premature and provisional."[119] Our true assessment of Chaucer seems similarly poised. We cannot assume that it has all been done; new material, and new thinking about old material, is all part of the adventure. The "God of English poets" deserves our best effort, a complete reevaluation.

V. A. Kolve's name, which has already been noted, is closely associated with new material and new thinking. His work provides a special access to medieval drama, and to Chaucer as well. We are generally unaware of the whole world of thought concerning faith, symbolism, and automatic stimuli to which Chaucer and his con-temporaries responded. Kolve, in his study of the Corpus Christi Play, demonstrates a rapport with the mentality behind the dramas, shows how their simple responses need to be part of our thinking, and presents a new interpretation which is nothing less than a breakthrough to the medieval psyche. He speaks of the dramatist who "guided the spectator in understanding the comedy as part of a coherent and reverent whole. The centuries that intervene be-tween his art and our experience of it have dimmed and partly muted his voice, but by attending to the nuances of his art, to the serious meaning behind the laughter, we can restore something of its original resonance."[120] Seeing comedy mingled with reverence, and seriousness behind the laughter will be a restorative to Chaucer as well. Chaucer's works and the Corpus Christi Play both grew out of fourteenth-century England.

In recent years Kolve has centered his interest on the *Canterbury Tales*. A study of the first five stories in proper medieval perspective has been called "the best and most important book on Chaucer to appear in twenty-five years"—a well-deserved recommendation. Kolve conveys the importance of the pictures in the mind that form while reading Chaucer's words. The poet was skilled at choosing words that elicited symbolic images that were spontaneously recognized by his audience. Kolve's work activates an inclusive base of inspirations beyond mere literature. Visual evidence in works of art could be a source for medieval literary themes and images. Kolve explains that "our pleasant task is double: we must educate our eyes to the period at large…and we must learn the symbolic language used in that period, sometimes in a fashion formally explicit, sometimes in a manner covered and complex."[121] If we limit our interpretations to the poet's words— without including the mental images he inspires—we limit the possibilities of interpretation. And we may be ignoring an entire level of his structure, of his intention.

Automatic responses of medieval churchgoers are often lost to us, such as the forms of address used for God, the implication of biblical names, the meaning behind church window images and intricate details in carvings that decorate the churches, the incidental information of everyday devotional activities. These were basic fibre of imagination for Londoners of the 1300s, but are not for ours. The fact is that "even ordinary members of Chaucer's audience would have known a whole repertory of [the medieval language of] signs; they saw them in paintings, carvings, and stained glass; they heard them explained as signs in sermons, confessional teaching, and didactic literature; and they heard them used, sometimes openly, sometimes in covered, ingenious ways, in narrative and lyric poems not primarily didactic in intent." These recognizable images were "one of the major vocabularies" for Chaucer's contemporaries. And it is Kolve's direct intent to provide us with a medieval mind-set, to "forward and assist" the "possibility of divergent readings"[122] of the *Canterbury Tales*—for those who have sufficient acquaintance with the life and common knowledge of Chaucer's day.

Along with the fine resource books to aid Chaucer discoveries, a new attitude toward, and interest in, the Middle Ages finds informative journal articles to provide necessary medieval background, or a stepping stone to new thinking. As intricate mental connections are disclosed it becomes progressively clearer that Chaucer's plan is anything but what was once called "crystalline simplicity." And his sophisticated medieval audience, aware of many areas of art and music and science and literature, were anything but "plodding ancestors." Life, even the life of medieval nobility, consisted of common, ordinary experiences as well; the day's ordinary activities too have their value and interest for medieval poets. *Sources and Analogues* of Chaucer's tales might give the impression that literary works beget more literary works, that no other insemination occurs. Hardly likely. There is a whole life to be lived and observed, while one's nose is not in a book.

It has been said that the poets of the richly complex and diverse Elizabethan world "wove ideas from everywhere into their pages." This supposition also seems a reasonable approach to Chaucer. In the charming lectures of John Livingston Lowes, he recalls the intimate dealings that Chaucer had with royal figures and clerics as well as soldiers and ditch diggers, concluding that "their roots are deep in the life [Chaucer] lived." For our poet, daily life and books "are indissolubly merged."[123] Then it is of the utmost importance to acquire a wide acquaintance with ordinary matters of late fourteenth-century daily life.

Through the centuries the world has gained a great deal of information, scientific facts, etc., but what each of us actually knows today is very compartmentalized, specialized. Chaucer's contemporaries understood their surroundings and dealt with them in a much more encyclopedic fashion. Their intimate acquaintance with the processes of birth and death, and the basics of daily survival was universal knowledge, necessary to both the high- and low-born. Remove our modern protective conveniences and scientific know-how and we would be challenged to cope with their "simple" lifestyle, to handle, for example, stresses of climate, disease, and sudden reversals of fortune. And the literature they enjoyed could incorporate this "encyclopedic" knowledge of living, to which we might be oblivious. Is it any wonder that some of Chaucer's phrases still mystify us? As we continue to pursue the image of Christ in the Host, we will discover words that are pregnant, but have hidden their condition until now. We will assist in the delivery of several as we learn (in the next chapter) to identify the fourteenth-century image of Christ.

Our respect for these medieval ancestors, who coped with their special complexities, is growing. And, as time goes on, we are also exhibiting a greater respect for the religious atmosphere of the time. A shallow reflection about forty years ago, regarding the Great Schism, said: "The spectacle of two popes, each claiming to be the vicar of Christ and each consigning the other to eternal damnation, was not edifying...."[124] "Not edifying," in reference to this spiritual torment, is like saying that the sinking of the *Titanic* was "a real shame." To trivialize the soul-rending catastrophe of the Schism is unthinkable today.

We have a greater awareness of the spiritual stresses of Chaucer's life as medieval sources inform us "that at the end of the century there was a spirit of lay devotion among courtiers and others which, whatever their sinful lives, showed a growth of sincere thought about religious truth." Some feel, and understandably so, that the many attacks of the plague were a major influence. Others who have studied the apocalyptic movement that spread across Northern France and Britain note that many were inspired to make calculations to determine the end of the world. The St. Paul's sermon spoke of the Anti-Christ, the world's end, and Judgment. Echoes of "prepare for Judgment" reflected on the ears and eyes and in the minds of fourteenth-century man, from frequent sermons to the "omnipresent art surrounding him during divine worship." Appreciating these pressures, we realize why the poet and many of his friends "had a taste...for serious writings on religion, philosophy and science."[125] Chaucer's serious interests are an integral part of the *complete* image of the man.

As we reinstate the poet's reputation as a man of faith, "we can see 'moral Chaucer'...if we open both eyes—the other eye got closed in the nineteenth century when people used to say that *The*

Canterbury Tales is notable for its bawdy and humorous presentation of human conduct." Now we know that "it is a shallow estimate of Chaucer's fun which fails to detect the underlying earnestness."[126] New concerns, freed from promoting religious discord, allow us to give full attention to the poetry.

G. K. Chesterton, once again, guides our approach to the religion of Chaucer's world: "Nobody can make head or tail of the fourteenth century without understanding what is meant by being a Catholic; and therefore by being a heretic." What Chesterton recommends is related to Kolve's purpose; we need to recognize the symbolism and values that guided fourteenth-century living and dying. But Chesterton indicates the essential dichotomy; the division commented on one hundred years ago was not accurate. The fourteenth-century person of faith who chose not to be Catholic was not a Protestant. If Chaucer asserted that he was not a Catholic he would be judged a *heretic*, and therefore guilty of what the Inquisitor Bernard Gui called "heretical depravity"—a grim consideration.[127]

If a man of deep faith wished to disguise a message, one method would be the clever use of ambiguities—as was Freewill's ploy in the poem mentioned earlier. Chaucer's purposeful use of ambiguity is gaining interest and respect as the following comparison will show. In 1968, when reference was made to a lengthy ambiguous passage (a three-hundred-thirty line description of the temple of Venus in the *House of Fame*), the reviewing author concluded that, whether we are to understand that the image of Venus is a sculpture or a painting, the description in question "is hardly clear—and it hardly matters." But when the same passage was examined in the 1980s another author was led to a different conclusion, "that the ambiguity is itself the answer. Chaucer would not have found it hard to be clear in such a description, had he wished."[128] Why the poet chose to be ambiguous, we don't know, but at least we are noticing and taking seriously what the poet chooses *not* to say. This will hold meaning as we see his poetry purposefully disclose a measured amount of information—but no more. Lack of clarity has its own meaning.

Another faith-connected choice is Chaucer's use of *pilgrimage* as his plan. Discernment of the basic unity of the *Canterbury Tales* sees the plan of *pilgrimage* profound and pervasive, rather than trivial or arbitrary. We may have overlooked a personal and intimate reference where the poet describes, "I lay ready to travel on *my* pilgrimage." The word *pilgrimage* itself had the quality of a "sacramental symbol" to Chaucer, not to be used lightly.[129] This idea of Chaucer's *personal* pilgrimage is thought provoking. It may be that the rest of the pilgrims are intended just as a meaningful enhancement to the poet's travels with the Host—with Christ—on his own life journey.

Further serious consideration, on Chaucer's part, immediately follows the last of the tales, the Parson's lengthy sermon. It is the poet's *Retraction*, a prayerful statement of attitude and purpose about his writings, that close the *Tales*. He beseeches his readers "pray for me that Christ have mercy on me and forgive me my offenses" and then lists his works "that sow into sin." He follows by thanking "our Lord Jesus Christ" for translations of good works, and concludes with hope "that I may be one of them, at the day of judgment, that shall be saved." This prayerful ending (the Parson's sermon and Retraction) may seem, to the twentieth-century reader, to come without sufficient preparation. For Chaucer and his contemporaries, it would pose no problem, but be accepted as "the mercurial nature of grace."[130] Man's spirit can be touched and respond in the "twinkling of an eye." But even if we see this prayer as a standard end-of-life gesture, this need not detract from our believing that it is a sincere expression of Chaucer's faith and hope.

As the twentieth century examines the *Retraction* and Chaucer's serious inclinations, it is refreshing to find unprejudiced speculations of the poet's deep faith. "Chaucer was not merely a courtly poet, or an ironist, or a moral teacher. He was moved instead by all those impulses to create an aesthetic design on the grandest and most generous scale, in which [the tales] could speak in complex counterpoint until the very end. There the deepest truths of a civilization are once again reaffirmed—to the aesthetic advantage of the work, certainly, in providing so authoritative a sense of closure, [the *Retraction*] but also, we may believe, in witness to the deepest beliefs of the author himself."[131] The poet stands before us as on hallowed ground. The image of *vulgar clown* is fading. We are able to grant his complex existence, his joy of living, his faith in his God.

The *Retraction* is a notable showing forth of Chaucer as a man of faith, who, with a simple medieval expression, sets straight his relationship with God and the world. This view of Chaucer may be the necessary preparation for being able to recognize Christ in our Host. I believe, for example, that Chaucer gives us direct evidence about the Host's personality. He is the overseeing judge of pilgrims—it is *we* who identify situations as ironic, comic, etc. From the beginning the Host said he would be the judge. In his final appearance he is solemn and commanding as he says to the Parson, "Hurry, the sun is setting."[132] He knows more than anyone that time is short. Seeing Chaucer as dwelling in "an age of faith" gives us the confidence to explore the more visionary readings of the *Tales* that have been proposed.

A reading of some depth was noted forty years ago when Speirs perceived that "the human comedy of the *Canterbury Tales* moves within an apprehension of an all-inclusive divine harmony." Apprehending a harmony that is divine tends toward seeing the pilgrims moving within the knowledge and pervasive power of God, or understanding the hand of God as the force that guides the action. God has been directly noted as "present throughout the *C[anterbury] T[ales]*," or as "Christ incognito under the features of these ill-assorted yet gloriously unific pilgrims."[133] This image comes from a Bible promise that had been meditated upon in Christian writings for centuries: where two or three are gathered in Christ's name, He is with them.

The representation of Christ joining pilgrims originates with the Bible account of the two disciples on their way to Emmaus. The poet's choice of *pilgrimage* can no longer be taken as a whim, a chance device. Where the traditional stimulation of spring was expressed as the greenery of nature, or the attraction of love, a different thought stirs Chaucer's heart to this penitential undertaking. A tentative proposal finds that "the pilgrimage, so elaborately launched, may exist for its own sake and not for the sake of becoming a cadre for the tales."[134] I see this skeletal structure as deliberate and dynamic symbolism. If the essence of the symbol remains unrecognized, however, the inner life of the poem lies dormant.

While in the past a great deal of time was spent by diligent researchers in discovering and displaying the "true" identity of several of the pilgrims—Henri Bayliff is an example—we are looking now for a different level of *truth*. The earlier search has served a purpose, but we now leave what has been taken to be *reality* and turn our steps toward the unknown—the hidden. We are "concerned with symbolic meaning—with the iconographic content of…mental images that are created by Chaucer's narrative and anchored in his audiences' memory."[135]

Acknowledging symbolic meaning can open our minds to new possibilities. The stories told are now often seen as confessions. If this is life's journey, with a penitential atmosphere and anticipation of judgment, then a confession from each pilgrim would be *appropriate*; perhaps *necessary* is the better word. The image of Christ in the Host is more visible if we take the tales to be *confessional*. Huppé plainly states, "The 'confessional' mood of the *Tales* is obvious, and many of the tales are in fact confessions, although some are imperfect ones." Speirs sees the admissions as more limited; the Wife and the Pardoner make confessions, but they differ "from those of the confessional" because they are "public" and the two pilgrims are "impenitent." What we really need is to gain a position where our mind's eye can get a comprehensive view, a view which sees that pilgrims making various kinds of confessions with varying degrees of sincerity and penitence lends *verismo* to the plan. All that Chaucer intended from the individual tales, characterized as "experiences that once happened,"[136] has yet to be seen.

Chaucer's readers know that these stories are told in anticipation of the Host's judgment; this atmosphere permeates the journey. As the symbolic importance of *one day* becomes clear, this author-imposed limitation comes into focus as the Day of Judgment. Explained allegorically, rather than realistically, Kolve perceives it as "a grander idea of pilgrimage, in which all human life is viewed allegorically as a pilgrimage toward death and God's just judgment."[137] Such an opinion would not have been possible one hundred years ago. Prevalent interpretation is not denied, but symbol/illusion is the adjunct, the connecting path to where the sentence—the hidden truth—is concealed. Comparing information from the *Tales* to what has been written about actual pilgrimages demonstrates a lack of reality.

> We do *not* have the return journey, not even the arrival at the shrine, but only a typological Pisgah sight from which the promised land can be seen but not reached before death. Hence we should understand, as readers did until the middle of the nineteenth century, that the journey takes place unrealistically in one day: the gathering darkness of the Parson's Prologue signals the end of the life of man.[138]

This historical information about perception of the time-element in Chaucer's pilgrim tales is not greatly circulated, but that does not diminish its importance.

Symbolism, we will see, holds answers that realism does not. We are being pushed to extend our self-imposed boundaries. Malone, thinking *realistically* in the 1950s, called the scheme of having thirty riders on the road all trying to hear each other's stories "obviously preposterous." It is, of course. But we must stretch our perception, not limit our thoughts to our experience in the real world. Imperfect reality might be splendid illusion. In the 1980s Howard viewed the same "preposterous" plan and found that "[Chaucer] violates our expectations...by withholding local color and circumstantial detail: we are not aware of horses, blessings, souvenirs or badges or trappings appropriate to pilgrims; there are no overnight stops, no cities are passed through, the destination is never reached.... The pilgrimage is eerily symbolic when you squint and see the whole." Chaucer, once again, provides only the details he wants his audience to have. It is up to us to set all the pieces in proper order. His "symbolic mode...uses a decoying realism to put the 'sentence seekers' off the scent."[139] Symbolism and illusion are the bridge to the sentence, his underlying message. Now that we are aware of the bridge, we need the courage to cross over.

Let's consider this "decoying realism" as it has been identified in the *General Prologue*. Relationships among the pilgrims, "the tempo of the dialogue...with its air of randomness and chatty ease, is in its way deceptive." The pilgrimage itself "with the repeated suggestion of mobility, is a *motif* that Chaucer expertly capitalizes upon." All the movement and liveliness we feel in the *General Prologue* is a bold deception, "ostensibly *en route*, [the pilgrims] have never left the hospice…. In the *Prologue*…there is no pilgrimage—but there is a mighty illusion of one."[140] Chaucer is a master at creating mental images, drawing pictures for us to see, and telling us *only* what he wants to tell. Without our realizing it, Chaucer withholds indications of time and place.

Another trick of his illusion has been called "designed vagueness"; it can be found when Chaucer fails—better yet *refuses*—to name the town just before the arrival of the pilgrims at their destination. The last *landmark* on the journey—the unnamed thorp (town)—is important for what Chaucer does not say. "The topographic reference *placing* the Parson's Prologue…is vague…such indeterminacy in this final link hints at a designed vagueness."[141] If a village or town had been named, there would be no doubt *where* the pilgrims were; they can only be in one tangible place. Instead, vagueness allows multiple interpretations. (Chaucer evidently delights in simultaneous interpretations.) The thorp was left nameless to create multilevel possibilities—one of which involves the undisclosed sentence.[142]

As references to symbolism and illusion are developing, there is even an openness toward associating the word *allegory* with Chaucer, though the association has problems. One of the tales (the Parson's) is said to be "an allegory of Penance, and of the inward meaning of the words of the Lord's Prayer." And when a critic finds Chaucer deficient in metaphors, we are told, nevertheless, that the poet's "similes…promote the visualization essential to allegorical vision." Elsewhere the reader is advised to try "thinking of the tales as either 'formally' or 'informally' allegorical," or as containing images that are "allegorical in potential," although it is claimed that the *Canterbury Tales* as a whole is "not an allegory in the formal sense."[143] Blinders are a thing of the Victorian past. We are much closer now to being able to see the actual allegories—look them in the eye, rather than turn away in distrust or embarrassment. What is needed, however, is a brave scholar who will formulate a vocabulary so that we will not be confused by terminology less than precise, as with allegories *formal, informal,* or *potential*.

Illusion has purpose; pictures communicate a symbolic level; images achieve response in memory. We need a store of fourteenth-century images in order to grasp the words firmly, instead of letting them slip away behind the screen of pseudo-realism we have raised. If we remove our preconceived limitations, gain a broader view, we discover a different idea of the whole. If we do not become distracted by the surface actions that are so life-like you can see them happening, we recognize how much *reality* is lacking, how symbolic Chaucer's overall plan becomes.

When much of early Chaucer criticism was published, a great deal of today's common knowledge had not yet been brought to light. Chaucer's words deserve reexamination now, as if we had never seen them before. His art form needs something other than scientific analysis. New insight comes from examining each word that falls out of place or trips us up. Continuing along the path, crossing the bridge that the twentieth century has constructed, gives promise of his words bringing us exciting discoveries ahead.

Absolutely devoid of any sense of historical perspective, the dramatist and his audience sought simply to realise the most sublime and sacred scenes of Scripture narrative. They felt no impropriety in impersonating the Deity on the stage...they introduced the most venerable personages in Scripture story feeling, acting, and speaking in a manner which everybody could understand.

—W. J. Courthope, A History of English Poetry (1895)

VII: What Are the Characteristics of the 14th-Century Image of Christ?

OUR TASK NOW will be to collect the information necessary to visualize the image of Christ that Chaucer would have identified, the picture fourteenth-century Englishmen held as sacred. The most important, and perhaps the most startling, fact about the image of Christ in medieval England is that He was very much like a fourteenth-century Englishman. If it seems, at first, that recognition should be easy, we need to remember that "we are no longer alive to...traditions" and "have lost the habits of mind" of the fourteenth-century church-goer.[144] We must temper our assumption of this being a simple task with some patience and humility.

Medieval lack of historical perspective has a quaint charm. Characters from Scripture behaved as those in comparable medieval positions, because it was understood that if "pretence has some signification, it is not a lie, but a figure of the truth." So Annas and Caiaphas might be portrayed in bishop's garb; Pilate could make references to "parliament" or call for the Bible to be consulted; and knights would guard Christ's Sepulchre.[145] Within dramas Christ was distinguished by what He said, how He said it and the circumstances of the action—recognizable situations patterned after Bible accounts. The Christ portrayed in dramas was identifiable to onlookers even when the other players "did not recognize" Him. And in poems, impressions of God (Christ) are expressed as everyday thoughts—lovingly, joyfully, fearfully, humbly.

But let's not get ahead of ourselves. These actors and stories were often participants of the Feast of Corpus Christi. The feast had been established about seventy-five years before the *Canterbury Tales* was begun. Dramas "celebrate in its fullest significance what the Middle Ages took to be the supreme gift of God, His Body for man's sin." The Eucharist, instituted by Christ a short time before the Crucifixion, had its significance overshadowed at Easter, because the Church was predominantly involved with commemoration of the Resurrection. And so, to give proper recognition for this transcendent Gift, a second separate feast was inaugurated and became the lavishly celebrated "principal feast of the church."[146] Special fraternities were formed within the Church to be in charge of these celebrations. (One such fraternity was established at St. Botolph's Church at Aldgate by the time Chaucer took up residence at Aldgate.) By adding this second feast, the Church wished the additional period of solemnity to demonstrate gratefulness to God for His extraordinary gift. No less a figure than Thomas Aquinas was commissioned by Pope Urban IV to write the special prayers for the commemorations.[147]

The constant presence of allegory "came to the people from the pulpit," and penetrated even the thinking of medieval theology. The many deep questions raised regarding the Real Presence of Christ—the "fragile, small wheaten disc [which became] God"— were analyzed and argued philosophically by some. But much of the medieval basis of instruction for priests combined "contemporary thinking and *traditional allegorical framework*." The enduringly influential treatise on the Eucharist, written by the man who would become Pope Innocent III, describes this gift as a divine mystery. Influence of this treatise can be found in the document establishing the Feast of Corpus Christi.[148]

The procession, mentioned earlier, has been a tradition of the Feast through the centuries and is, even today, throughout the Catholic world. Kolve, once again, gives historic insight: "The Eucharist serves to recall both the Last Supper and the flesh and blood of Christ offered on the cross—events about which it is possible to rejoice only when they are related to man's fall, Christ's Resurrection, and the Last Judgment. Except for this sacrifice and gift, even the good would have been damned, guilty of Adam's sin."[149]

Though some have questioned the value or meaning of taking the Sacramental Bread out of the church building and carrying it through the town, a simple explanation has been offered: "There is surely nothing more extraordinary in the Host being carried ceremonially out of the Sanctuary and into the streets and squares of a town than in the attempt by mortal men to make visible the miracle of the Resurrection by personifying it in the Sanctuary[.] Yet what else can the presence of the Host in the market place signify if not the determination that the former should sanctify the latter?"[150] The explanation seems appropriately medieval, and we may ask if this was not also Chaucer's intention—that the Host should sanctify the final work of his life, his pilgrimage?

An interesting feature of the processions would be the pauses made at water conduits as out-of-door stations, where hymns could be sung and blessings given. When plays became part of the celebration, performers used the large (often circular) stone structure of the conduit as a stage.[151]

The subject of the plays is "human history and God's interventions in it." Throughout the day-long festivities many stories would be told of God's involvement with mankind, starting with Adam and Eve and ending with Judgment. And Kolve makes a surprising but penetrating observation about the "central episode": Christ's Passion and death is "joyful in meaning."[152] Adam's sin is a happy fault because it was the reason that Christ gave His life for man. God, the Father, so generous and forgiving, gave His Son to save men from hell. The beginning of the Annunciation play (Towneley) finds God the Father declaring that Redemption be put in motion; Adam and Eve had been "beguiled...through the serpent":

> But yet I mean to grant [Adam] grace,
> And the oil of mercy for his gain,
> And in time to ease his pain.
> For he has suffered sin full sore,
> For these five thousand years and more,
> First on earth and then in hell;

> But long therein he shall not dwell.
> Beyond pain's power he shall be laid,
> I will not lose what I have made.
> I will make redemption,
> As promised, in my person,
> All with reason and with right
> Both through mercy and through might.
>
> · · ·
>
> Righteousness will we perform;
> My son shall take on human form,
>
> · · ·
>
> And I intend that prophecy
> Be here fulfilled by me.[153]

Through the Father's power and mercy, man will be saved by His devoted Son. A medieval image of Christ describes Him coming out of the world with bloody clothes *as if He is the king of joy.*[154] The joy contained in Christ's suffering and death is that man, once doomed, was now destined for everlasting bliss.

An actor portraying the Soul of Christ, *Anima Christi*, appears in the Coventry play, nine lines after Christ's death on the cross, and counsels his listeners:

> Now all mankind in heart be glad
> with all mirth that may be had
> for man's soul that was afflicted
>   in the camp of hell;
> now shall rise to live again
> from pain to place of pure paradise
> Therefore man in heart be joyful
>   in mirth now shalt thou dwell.[155]

Man's source of everlasting joy is the obedient death of Christ.

In the following prayer taken from the *Divine Office* (the official prayer of the Church said by the clergy each day) for the Corpus Christi Feast, we are given a summation of the meaning of Christ to the Christian.

By His birth He became man's *companion;*
at this *supper* He became man's *food;*
in His death He became man's *price;*
in His kingdom He becomes man's *prize.*[156]

Words I've emphasized hold Christ's dominant images for medieval man.

Such images elicited many titles for addressing their Savior. Inventiveness of authors would often take these titles and create a dramatic action for the plays, perhaps like medieval "charades." Examples might be "prince of peace" or "healer of men." (I wonder whether *poets* used the same inspiration for presenting images in their writings, the action being described in verse rather than dramatized.) Some actions might have a natural comic element but Kolve recommends that we attune ourselves to the medieval mindset: "however funny, bumptious, coarse, or improvisatory these comic actions may seem, they have their roots in serious earth; they are intimately and intricately involved in their play's deepest meanings."[157] If comedy brought the correct image to the onlooker's mind, the writer's task had been accomplished. This is a thought to be recalled when we examine action in Chaucer's plan.

There was a long history of the commemoration of the pilgrim episode in the Bible where two of the disciples travel to Emmaus after the Crucifixion. St. Gregory the Great (d. 604) considered the Emmaus journey "the quintessential exemplum of the pilgrim life." The exemplum was often presented as a drama (the *Pilgrim Play*) on Easter Monday. The disciples, traditionally Luke and Cleophas, on the road to Emmaus, encounter Christ. He joins them as they walk, but He is not recognized by them. Influence of the Emmaus episode demonstrates the medieval resonance of the word *pilgrimage.* St. Augustine of Hippo (d. 430) "associates the Emmaus story again with mankind's journey, first remarking that 'all men joined to Christ by faith and love are *on the way,*' and then reasoning that 'since Christ and his members are one, then Christ, like all men, is a journeyer.'" On this journey the godly and the ungodly "live side-by-side, and even intermingle."[158] They travel together though their ultimate destinations differ. These, and many other ideas of Augustine's, echo through the centuries.

We know that the Emmaus story was dramatized in churches of England, France, and Italy, being presented to the congregation in Latin. The tradition in England, however, changed from Latin to English portrayals. Christ and the pilgrims became "colloquial in speech and gesture," and then the action was moved outdoors where the performances took on a "'new' realism as the audience apprehends characters recognizably appropriate to the English countryside." Christ, in these English *peregrini*, is seen as a "provocative commentator."[159] *Provocative commentator* would also be an apt description of Chaucer's Host; and characters who travel outdoors, and are appropriate to the English countryside, bring to mind the Canterbury Pilgrims. Chaucer's imagination certainly could have gained inspiration while a witness to the "new realism" of pilgrim plays spoken in English.

Many used this pilgrim Scripture as inspiration. The theme is found in a sermon by St. Bernard, whose main concern, however, is the Risen Christ. He prompts Christians to "choose whether you, with Mary Magdalen, desire to see Jesus in the form of a gardener, or, with the co-disciples, *as a pilgrim*."[160] In a meditative, or perhaps an eschatological sense, Christians were encouraged to see Christ in their midst as a pilgrim.

When the onlookers saw the three pilgrims in the English countryside, it became a dramatization (the identifiable charade) of "where two or three are gathered in my name, I am with them." Relevance to daily life was easily grasped by the viewers because Christ and His friends were much like their neighbors in their words and actions—and in point of fact, they *were* their neighbors.

Christ was the major force in the faith of Chaucer's countrymen. This may seem an obvious statement, but the fact needs to be established because England's religious focus differed from that of the Continent—especially France. (For example, during the fourteenth century, the French developed a kind of drama called *Miracles of Our Lady* "of which no counterpart ever existed in England.") Chaucer's homeland did not participate in what has come to be called "the Cult of the Virgin." There was "no exaggerated reverence for the Mother of God." Instead, what prevailed as "*the principal theme of Middle English poetry from the earliest times might be said to be the Passion*"[161] and devotion to Christ's Holy Name. A typical prayer is:

> Jesus, for Thy Holy Name,
> And for Thy bitter Passion,
> Save me from sin and shame
> And endless damnation.[162]

Two popular lines inserted in many prayers, which indicates they were "widely and orally known," are:

> Lord, for Thy Holy Name
> Shield me from the world's shame.[163]

Short prayers of this sort could be found "through every work in Middle English!" Rubin's study indicates that Christ's suffering and its implications were the source of popular devotions, and confirms the special devotion to the Name of Jesus in prayers and exempla with special "English flavour." Chaucer's Parson displays a like reverence for *Jesus* as the only name that has power to save, and instructs "how precious is the name of Christ." Chaucer also dramatized this devotion in *The Man of Law's Tale*.[164]

Christ, in many guises, surrounded Chaucer and his contemporaries—in poems, sermons, plays, in stone, glass, and illuminations of manuscripts. Prayers to the Holy Name and Christ's Passion, thoughts of Christ the Redeemer and the gift of the Eucharist were the center of religious life. Twentieth-century research gives us assurance of Christ's dominance.

From the 1200s onward there was a special emphasis upon the *humanity* of Christ. Dominican and Franciscan preachers told men that God was "acquainted with suffering through the pain of Christ on the Cross." (Unrelieved pain was part of medieval life.) It was also the time in history when the Bethlehem scene, the crèche we know so well, was introduced to Christmas imagery. The Gospel scene was brought to life—the ox and ass and the tiny baby in the manger—for men to experience. Christ was shown coming into the world helpless, as do all men.[165]

Early dramatists represented the Deity acting and speaking just as their neighbors might. The medieval figure of Christ could walk along a road, travel with pilgrim disciples, or turn to the townsfolk, who made up the audience, and lead them in singing the *Te Deum*, a hymn of joy.[166]

The dramatized presence of Christ in fourteenth-century England was an occasional occurrence. But of all the representations of Christ in Chaucer's world, the most prominent and ever-present expression was the Real Presence in the Consecrated Host of the altar, often spoken of as a banquet (as it still is today). Poetically expressed:

> His flesh is our fair feast
>
> . . .
>
> Almighty God omnipotent
> His blessed body has sent
> To feed his friends here.[167]

In a poem by John Lydgate, called "A Procession of Corpus Cristi," he describes the sacrament.

> Fruit celestial hangs on the tree of life,
> The fruit of fruits for a certainty,
> Our help, our food, and our restorative
> And chief repast of our redemption.[168]

If the images "fruit hung on the tree" and "our repast" seem to merge the figure of Christ with the food that is eaten, this is intentional. The Bread is identified as Christ.

This *food* was (and generally is even today) small, flat, circular unleavened wafers called *hosts* from the Latin *hostia*, meaning *victim*; victim, because Christ had died for man. This food is the "well-being of the world," it gives strength, makes men whole again.[169] The Eucharist was seen as the "bread of life," necessary food for the journey:

> With superior meat he nourished mankind,
> For with his flesh he did me feed;
> A better food may no man find,
> For to everlasting life it will us lead.[170]

A section of Lydgate's *Pilgrimage of the Life of Man* is presented as Christ's last will and testament. Jesus declares:

> My Body I leave also
> To true pilgrims that go,
> As the thing that will them most avail
> To relieve them in their travail (or *travel*)
> As chief Repast, to sustain them[171]

Fourteenth-century faith affirmed that "the centre of the religious acts of the day was the priest's turning bread and wine into the body of God."[172] Importance of the Eucharistic Presence cannot be overemphasized.

Lesson V from the *Divine Office* for the Feast of Corpus Christi celebrates:

> O banquet most precious! O banquet most admirable! O saving banquet overflowing with every spiritual delicacy! Can anything be more excellent than this repast? ...Christ the true God is given us for nourishment.[173]

An antiphon for the day speaks of "the Bread of Christ"[174] that nourishes.

And the wine that would accompany this excellent repast comes from the cask hung upon a tree:

> With his flesh thy spirit is fed;
> He gave his healing cask
> To make his good banquet guests glad,
> With spear of very sharp point;
> Then was found a fatal faucet,
> In the tree cask it was set,
> Christ's heart was pierced and drained,
> His breast was all drained of blood.[175]

Almighty God provides a complete banquet in the Eucharistic Service.

Terms in "A Prayer to the sacrament" commemorate "bread of life," "holy host," "true sacred flesh," "true man," "our joy," and "mirth of heart," reflecting with simplicity medieval man's sense of appreciation. This Host was given as sustenance and joy for the world. John Wyclif's attempts to discourage belief in the Real Presence in the 1380s was met by "bristling indignation" from some of those who were believers.[176]

Though the fact of changing bread and wine into the Body of Christ occurred during the Mass each day, men were traditionally bound to receive it only once a year. (This will be an issue as we look at the activities of Chaucer's pilgrims.) Preparation for reception of God's Body would mean going to confession, cleansing one's soul. *The Lay Folks Catechism* instructs "the sacrament of the altar, / Christ's own body in likeness of bread, / ... / [each man and woman] / ought to receive once in the year, / that is to say, at Easter." *Festivals of the Church* advises that "Easter is our perfect food."[177] At the Paschal celebration each person was to partake of the best of food. Other fourteenth-century words may intend a similar reference saying, "vitaille (victuals) at the best."

Having established the importance of Christ and the Eucharist, let's look at traditional qualities of His portrayal. Evidence comes from His own statements, from homage of others and even in third-person references to Himself. Easter Monday had a tradition mentioned briefly above, the reenactment of the two disciples on the way to Emmaus joined by Christ, who appeared as another pilgrim. In the Coventry version of the drama, He asks "to walk in fellowship" with Luke and Cleophas. Luke replies, "Welcome, in God's name! We say not nay." As they walk, the disciples recall Christ's recent death. Christ, speaking in the third person, encourages:

> Be merry and glad with heart full free
> For of Christ Jesus that was your friend
> Ye shall have tidings of game and glee.[178]

The anonymous Wakefield dramatist has Jesus explain, again in the third person, "wherever is game and play: / Of that mirth shall he never miss." The disciples cannot accept their companion's joyful words, which causes Christ to scold:

> Heed what prophecies avow,
>   Which are not vain.
> Told they not what wise and how
>   That Christ should suffer pain?
>   .   .   .
>
> They said Jesus to death should go,
>   And be tortured on rood (the *cross*);
>   .   .   .
>
> His wounds running with red blood;
>   .   .   .
>
> Christ behooved to suffer this,
>   For sooth, right as I say,
> And after enter to his bliss.[179]

Christ is forthright—critical, instructive, joyful, man's companion. But not until the breaking of the bread at their evening meal will His identity finally be revealed.

A poignant fourteenth-century lyric, a dialogue between Jesus and his mother at the Cross, also presents Christ speaking in the third person:

> Maiden and mother, come and see,
> thy child is nailed to a tree;
> hand and foot he is unable to move,
> his body is wounded (or *twisted*) all in woe.[180]

In the above examples, Christ instructs, and challenges those around Him while speaking truth about Himself under cover of the third person. If we should find Chaucer's Host speaking *of* Christ, we must remember that this cannot be taken as a clear indication that he is *not* Christ.

The medieval concept of God's omnipotence, His "unlimited freedom," is clearly shown: "God, in His majesty, may do whatsoever He pleases." Popes and royalty are humble before Him. In the Chester Play of the *Last Judgment*, for example, a pope says, "Lord I must revere thee / ... / for thou art greatest in majesty." A queen addresses Christ as "Peerless Prince of greatest power," and a king refers to Him as "Lord of lords, and King of kings...thy power, lord, spreads and springs."[181] The world's most powerful persons address Christ as immeasurably more powerful than they. He is seen as forceful, dominating.

Chaucer and his contemporary playgoers knew that Christ had been born to die, and recognized as the most important aspect of Christ's death that He, "the godhead went into hell, / And harrowed it." This harrowing released the souls of the just, freeing them to the bliss of paradise. Christ, the Savior never stained by sin, storms the gates of hell and defeats Satan—the consummation of God's salvific plan. In the poem, *The Harrowing of Hell*, Satan, out of habit, identifies Jesus as a sinner because He is in hell, but the devil is swiftly silenced when Jesus asserts, "You never found sin *in* me as in another man."[182] Though it was foretold that Christ would take upon Himself all the sinfulness of mankind, sin, nevertheless, is not part of His being.

His language and actions show Him forceful. Christ can be harsh and direct, as in His portrayal in *Cursor Mundi*:

> Clearly spoke he what he would
> and his skill wisely he told.
> In his reproaching he was awful.[183]

Once again we find an outspoken, jibing Savior. Part of Christ's medieval personality is explosive, critical and outspoken, and exemplified by angry outbursts on stage. Pilgrims receive harsh words; said to Luke and Cleophas, the words touch each member of the audience, as well:

> Ye fools, ye are not stable!
> Where is your wit, I say?
> Both bewildered and unable
> To reckon the right way,
> For believe it is no fable
> That has befallen this same day.[184]

It is His recognizable role—and His words are an expected purgative for the audience. When He is seen ridding the temple of money-changers, He comes into the scene *"cum flagello"* (with a scourge); He strikes and scatters those who have been misusing His Father's house. Elsewhere, He denounces as "wretches" a crowd of Jews who have found a woman guilty of adultery; He chides others as "fools and feeble." Lastly, in a poem about the Harrowing, at hell's gate He shouts, "Where is the gateman? / I take him to be a coward." The frightened devil complains, "I have heard hard words / ... / I'll leave the gates and run away."[185]

In addition to harsh words, men of the Middle Ages questioned the cursing and swearing frequently done by God. (Check any Bible concordance.) If it was a proper thing to do, why were men forbidden to do so? If God did it, how could preachers tell church-goers it was wrong? Owst tells of a witty homilist who explained to his congregation that "if thou hast intelligence equal to God's in wit, and power and wisdom, then you might swear as God did."[186] The speech of God, of Christ, could be harsh, cursing, condemning, as part of the medieval image.

In recent years, an intriguing discovery was made about a form of creative swearing; the incoporation of oaths may have a deeper purpose than understood before. Maynard Mack, Jr., did a close reading of the jolly Christmas parody, *The Second Shepherd's Play*, a farce paralleling the Christ Child with a stolen sheep. The dialogue of the shepherds involves a great deal of swearing. What Mack discovered was that "the *full* drama of Christ's life has been revived for us in the oaths that recur at every turn, from his birth…to the Cross…to the risen Savior."[187] What a revelation! As the parody is being played out, an audible overlay of the particulars of Christ's life is flung into the ears of those listening. The bawdy shepherds were "unaware" that they were recalling Jesus' whole life for the audience, but the dramatist was not unaware. How often was this technique—chaste intention of apparent crudity—used? Let's be alert to such possibilities.

We have seen a number of characteristics identified with the fourteenth-century Christ—omnipotence, sinlessness, harshness, inclination to curse and swear. Now let's look at the roles He was given to play, in addition to that of pilgrim/journeyer.

Christ's Crucifixion was the victory of a hero, the Savior Knight, a Warrior against Satan. In a fourteenth-century lyric Christ says of the Cross, "My palfrey is made of a tree." In the drama of the Crucifixion the torturers say to Christ, "We shall set thee in thy saddle"; "Stand near, fellows, and let us see / How we can horse our king so free." And one torturer says to another, "I hope he and his palfrey / Shall not part this night."[188]

Stage directions in the Crucifixion and Last Judgment are quite detailed. Angels stand holding the instruments of torture and death: a cross, a crown of thorns, a lance, and other implements. Instructions describe "blood is emitted from His side," and Christ, dying on the cross, says to *all* attending the Towneley performance, "I thus for thee have bled."[189] The outspoken Christ often recalls details of His death.

Medieval prayer exhibited a strong interest in the Passion; we noted earlier that this was central to English medieval religious thought. Many poems and prayers, collected by Brown, depict Christ alluding to his Crucifixion:

> All…for thy sake
>
> . . .
>
> The nails, the scourges, and the spear,
> The gall, and thorns sharp—
> All these will witness bear
> That I have thee abiding in my heart.

Christ, appealing to man, says:

> Behold my side,
> my wounds spread wide,
> Restless I ride.
> Look up at me!…

In another, Christ speaks of His mercy:

> Man, I love thee above all things,
> And for this love would I hang,
> My blessed blood to bleed.

And, with elements compressed:

Tormented, nailed and done on a tree—
All, man, for love of thee.

Poetry also expresses joy in spite of pain:

The crown of joy, under thorns lay.

and:

Sweet be the nails,
and sweet be the tree,
and sweeter be the burden that hangs upon thee!

With such details of pain and agony it may be difficult to remember that Christ's Passion and death was a joyful event. The moment is memorialized in a lyric as Christ says:

On the cross I hang for man's sake,
This game I alone must play.[190]

Though these playful words seem strange and out of place today, they were accepted and cherished by Christians of Chaucer's day.

This hero of mankind, when the game had been played out, descended to hell to be the hero of those who had long awaited release. The non-biblical *Gospel of Nicodemus* describes the Hero's arrival at the gate of hell:

A voice spoke then terrifyingly,
    as if it were a thunder's blast:
"undo your gates at once, bid I,
    they may no longer last,
The king of bliss comes in through you."

But the forces of hell are foolish enough to hesitate, so:

Then Jesus struck so fast,
The gates went asunder
And iron bands all burst.

Prophets of old had said "how he would harrow hell" (release the righteous souls).[191] The Christ of Chaucer's day was anything but mild-mannered and soft-spoken. Christ valiantly vanquishes Satan. He is a bold, heroic knight.

We'll look at two other heroic representations of Christ, one well known Old English, much anthologized; the other lesser known fourteenth-century, extremely visual. First, from "Dream of the Rood," the Cross—the Rood—is speaking:

> Then the young Warrior,   God, the All-Wielder,
> Put off His raiment,   steadfast and strong;
> With lordly mood   in the sight of many
> He mounted the Cross   to redeem mankind.
> When the Hero clasped me   I trembled in terror.[192]

The structure of the fourteenth-century lyric, the second heroic representation, is a lengthy question followed by Christ's reply:

> What is he, this young lord that comes from the fight
> With blood-red garments so fiercely clothed,
> So well-attired, so handsome to the sight,
> So steadfastly goes, so brave in combat, this knight?
>
> It is I, it is I, that speaks naught but right,
> Champion to save mankind in the fight.[193]

Christ is powerful—the strong, aggressive champion of mankind. Nails, blood, and all are declarations of the extent of Christ's love, His obedience to His Father, His willingness to give Himself to save mankind.

A second role identified with Christ is that of *Guide.* Jesus says to Peter in one of the plays, "I shall go before, / That your going I may guide."[194] And He says to His mother:

> Man's soul that I loved ay, I shall redeem surely,
> Unto bliss of heaven for ay, I shall bring it to me.[195]

And the last example is an exchange between the pilgrims, Lucas and Cleophas. The gist of the conversation, from the unknown dramatist of York, is thought-provoking:

> Lucas: That lord who has lent me this life for to lead,
>   In my ways mayst thou guide me
>
>   .   .   .
>
>   Let us therefore tarry at no town
> Cleophas: At towns for to tarry take we no intent,
>   But take leisure at this time to talk of some
>   tales.[196]

It is surprising to note their intention of stopping at no towns, and an agreement to tell tales; both ideas parallel the Canterbury pilgrimage. Ultimately, of course, we can see this as an allegory of life as pilgrims move forward in time inexorably, no turning aside, no stopping, no turning back.

For now, let's complete our view of life (with its guide) as a pilgrimage. Augustine's influence can be seen in the Canterbury pilgrims, as both the godly and ungodly travel together although their eternal destinations differ. And for the reader, it has been suggested by the writings of St. Gregory that, "the experience of reading a [pilgrimage] commentary is itself...an enactment of the pilgrim life."[197] Did Chaucer, whose Parson often quotes this St. Gregory, see his readers joined with him in his own pilgrimage of life?

And what is it that man anticipates at the end of life's journey? Judgment. The fourteenth-century picture of Judgment is carved over the western portal of many churches; the western portal is meaningfully chosen because it faces the setting sun. Christ, the Judge, is enthroned, and surrounded by a microcosm of the scene of Doomsday: the Archangel Michael holding the scales of Justice, the dead rising from their graves and clearly separated into two groups—the Good escorted to the bosom of Abraham, the Damned being thrust into the mouth of hell, with depictions of their torments—a full complement of angelic messengers on one side and hellish tormentors on the other. Verbally it is "the mighty Lord's great day," that "surpriseth suddenly / careless mortals bound in sleep."[198]

Mortals bound in sleep are to be wakened by Christ, a duty

with which He is charged. A charming legend in *Cursor Mundi* explains, with an allegory comparing Christ to a lion:

> Lion may he rightly be called,
> For there may not be a mightier beast.
> And there is another reason
> Why he is designated as a lion,
>
> .   .   .
>
> Of the lion also the nature is that he,
> Sleeping never closes his eyes,
> Nor Jesus, though his ghost he yield
> His godhead that has power over all,
> Might never die nor never shall,
> Nor sleep, that *has to wake us all*. [199]

Like the lion's, Christ's eyes never close; they are always wide-open. For now, this is a curious little allegory, but Christ's eyes will be of considerable importance as we examine Chaucer's Host.

As we consider the end of man's pilgrimage and being wakened for Judgment, the very end of man's path demands a reckoning. The eternal decision is expressed as an accounting. First, man's Redemption was "bought" with Christ's blood. To be *bought* means to be redeemed from sin, as prayers frequently refer to man *bought* "on Rood" (on the Cross) and Christ the "*forbyer*," the Redeemer. [200]

Judgment of each soul is an individual reckoning, as in Scripture, "The kingdom of heaven is like a king that would reckon with his servants." The sermon at St. Paul's repeatedly warns that the time is close to give "reckoning of thy bailiwick"; each person is called to "yield reckoning" at the Doom (the Judgment). [201] *Cursor Mundi* speaks of our debt, but this concern is not with our having been "bought," but with the fact that:

> each of us clearly
> Hath received [from] God's treasury
> Excellent coins (talents) of gold they are
> Some have less and some more to look after
> Those coins are ours so that we plan
> That we may well pay our debt

On account…

> . . .

> He gives us grace so to account
> That we may to heaven mount.[202]

The understanding is that men are indebted to God for all they have received from Him. At Judgment, then, man must justify what has been done with each of his gifts, as with the biblical servants who received the talents.

Reckoning means rendering an account, or making atonement for one's life, to God at death or judgment. The Chester play of the Last Judgment refers to "*reckoning* of the right," and elsewhere to those who "*reckon* their deeds" before Christ, their Judge. In staging the general Judgment in a Morality Play, an essential of the plot is each soul, approaching Death's door, grasps a personal balance sheet.[203] It is a commonplace that terms which appear to allude to money are also standard terminology of Judgment.

Preaching about Judgment used the same expressions. Owst tells of an example in which many of the dead were assembled for Judgment. One soul "must render account," then the soul "who follows him, confesses" his misdeeds.[204] The terms *render account* and *confess* are interchangeable, synonymous. It would be difficult to think Chaucer would not have noticed the reciprocal relationship.

The same confession/accounting relationship is found again in Gower's *Confessio Amantis*, where the double image is doubly effective. Gower tells us that at our last Day of Account man will come before "Christ the Auditor."[205] Words said of a bookkeeping ritual before the Examiner have two faces, look in two directions. As an alternate to the money-related view, the "Day of Account" can also mean a *day of narration*; and Christ as the Auditor can be the celestial *Listener!* One view is a ledger and reviewer (account/auditor), but another vantage point sees a confession and listener (account/auditor). Is this Chaucer's ambiguous plan for the accounts presented by the pilgrims to the listening Host?

And what is the longed-for result of the reckoning, the accounting? "Joy and endless mirth." Referents to joy are regular companions to Christ, who is man's "mirth of heart." Christ is "the first cause of bliss." He explains, "My Father sent me from bliss to earth for mankind's sake." At Chester He proclaims, "I bled to bring you bliss." *Cursor Mundi* calls Him "the king of bliss," and when Christ confronts the devil, He identifies Himself as "A King of Bliss, who is called Jesus." Mirk's instructions for priests tells that Jesus rose to "glad us all" and "maketh us mirth." Those who have lived good lives, or have atoned for their sins, look forward to everlasting mirth, to being surrounded by bliss.[206] As the *Lay Folks Catechism* says,

> If we do well while we are here
> Wend with God to that bliss that evermore lasts.
> And if we do evil, to endless pain.[207]

Bliss and *mirth* correspond to the joy of heaven.

Let's give a final glance at Judgment, just enough to note that it is often spoken of as "the Lord's great day," and "Day of Account." *Cursor Mundi* exhorts:

> The day of Doom men call it
>   .   .   .
> Whether it lasts a short while or long.[208]

There is a picture in the medieval mind of Judgment taking place on *one day*.

We have now reached our last consideration—Christ's fourteenth-century wife. In *The Stanzaic Life of Christ*, entries for Lent speak of her *widowhood*. For Sexagesima Sunday *The Golden Legend* alludes to "widowhood...and her sorrow in the absence of her Spouse."[209] But a more intriguing situation is found in *Gesta Romanorum* in a piece entitled, "Of Three Questions Asked by Our Lord." It begins:

> Our Lord put three questions to His spouse, and said "I am thy maker and thy lord; tell me three things that I ask of thee."[210]

He questions, and after listening to her replies, He instructs her as to how she might improve. The importance here is that Christ is pictured with a wife; if Chaucer chose to present the same picture, it would not be out of place. Christ's wife, who is questioned, is not perfect, and neither is Goodelief, the Host's wife.

So this is the image of Christ in the fourteenth century. He is important first of all in the Eucharist, a banquet, the nourishment for mankind's journey through life. He is associated with joy, heroism, and omnipotence in the Passion, Crucifixion, Resurrection, and Judgment Day. Jesus is the sinless Savior who took all of man's sins upon Himself. His overwhelming victory in the harrowing of hell is a vivid medieval characterization. The roles Christ plays are many: man's hero; man's champion who bought salvation with His own blood; the destroyer of the gates of hell, who released the penitent souls to their blissful reward. He is the Guide of pilgrims, and man's Judge who will examine each account as reckoner/listener. And though of lesser importance—details such as speaking of Himself in the third person; reproaching in an explosive, outspoken manner; having eyes that are always open; being married to a wife of whom He is critical—all help to complete the picture.

I do not claim that the many sources of Christ-images mentioned above were specifically known by Chaucer. What the images do demonstrate, however, is that the characterizations are a general *recognizable* picture of Christ present in the minds of the people of Chaucer's England.

And now the moment is at hand to speculate about this image of Christ. Is it reflected in Geoffrey Chaucer's Host?

I wish now to bring together evidence from several different areas of medieval thought, all of which converges upon one central fact.... The progress of my argument for a time must become something other than linear: we shall have to make several independent journeys from the circumference to the center, reaching each time a similar conclusion, but in a sequence that I trust will become steadily richer and more comprehensive.

—V. A. Kolve, *Chaucer and the Imagery of Narrative (1984)*

VIII: Does Chaucer's Host Fit This Image of Christ?

THIS IS THE moment we've been building toward. Chaucer's words are about to lead us down a covered path, a path not much traveled in recent years. They will provide the light; it will be our job to keep our eyes—and our minds—open. If an unexpected figure appears on the path, know that it means no harm to you—nor to Chaucer.

We will compare qualities of the Host with Chaucer's statements about Christ; and, where there are no words of Chaucer's to guide us, we will look to the fourteenth-century image just presented; and, if need be, we will call upon additional medieval sources to quicken our response. We'll begin by confronting what can be the two strongest objections to a Host/Christ image: his hard (blasphemous?) language; and his role as literary critic, rather than seeing him as Judge. A detailed look at his initial description in the *General Prologue* will follow. Then, considerations of his interaction with the pilgrims will provide a deeper understanding of their guide, the Host. Lastly, we will examine intriguing "facts" of the journey.

Our goal is to gain a view of the Host and pilgrims which senses that "the various paths of the Tales are confronted with the Way; the many features of truth gaze on Truth itself; and the inner lights of the several pilgrims behold the Light." The conclusion, touched upon earlier is that, "God is present throughout the *C[anterbury] T[ales]*."[211] Chaucer's words, his faithful retainers, who were charged long ago, are about to reveal their secret mission. What has been a game of chance—now, with enhancements from the twentieth century—is becoming a game of skill; a new set of rules, I'm sure, will be forthcoming. This is an opportunity to participate in the recreation of the poem. But we must be on guard not to let pass apparently dull words that come our way; it may be that we only need to renew their gloss so that we will be allowed to secure their confidence.

If we read to derive a serious, hidden intention, and value the potential of inventive allegory, Chaucer's words will be able to bestow access to secret passages. We can see his Host as "domineering...lord of all he surveys"[212] and attribute his dominant personality to be part of the amusement (because the Host is a pompous innkeeper), but, in seeking the double meaning, we will also find his dominance appropriate (because the Host is the image of God). Many clues will be offered which lead to the confirmation of the Host as Christ—but, ultimately, it will depend on what you choose to see, as Chaucer's words demonstrate their subtle strategies.

Let's begin with a brief glimpse at Chaucer's own picture of Christ. Just prior to the introduction of the Host, the poet expresses an important detail regarding his personal image of Christ. He says, "Christ himself spoke very broadly (freely) in holy writ / And you well know it is no villainy."[213] Chaucer expects Jesus to speak freely, and when He does, it is not shameful or wicked. *Our* concept of the way Christ would speak is not the concern here. It is *Chaucer's* mental image that needs to be seen; and that need is twofold.

First, Christ will be presented as a person speaking broadly— freely or frankly. It would work at cross-purposes to think this refers to language that is less than outspoken, less than offensive; we are being cautioned about verbal content. And why this stated caution, if *broad* were to be taken mildly? Characterizations of Christ in the dramas certainly spoke freely—chastising, criticizing, demanding justice.

The second need, in order to shape proper expectations, is to see the statement from the reverse point of view, as if it were another signal: the one who is presented speaking broadly, the one who *is* the "explosive swearer,"[214] is portrayed in this way in order to indicate Christ, as Chaucer sees Him. Frankness, and free use of expletives is a clue, an affirmation of Chaucer's Christ image, an aid to our identifying Him. We will take note of the Host's carefully chosen words further on. For now, Chaucer's description of Christ coincides with the portrayal of God (in the Bible and medieval dramas) concerning strong language. We need only take the Host's words as simple and direct, assuming (on a level of hidden meaning) neither pervasive comedy, nor blasphemy.

In addition to the Host's bold language, a second opinion which could keep a reader from having an open mind is believing that Chaucer meant the Host to be a literary critic. If we limit ourselves to Chaucer's words, however, he associates only *judgment* with the Host's proposal: the pilgrims will "stand at my judgment." The literary critic image is part of poking fun at the Host; once he is declared a literary critic, then some will say, "his literary opinions need not be taken...seriously."[215]

In the actual history of criticism in fourteenth-century England, rhetoric, philosophy, and theology were considered important—literature was a mere hand-maiden. It seems reasonable to agree with Spurgeon that "no criticism was for us possible until the pre-eminence of Chaucer's work had helped to establish the dialect of London as the standard English speech, and until we possessed a certain body of literary work, both in prose and verse, which could be analyzed, commented on and compared." The printer, Caxton, one hundred years after the *Tales*, was the first to express critical literary opinions. And "the art of printing had been invented and exercised for a considerable time, in most countries of Europe, before the art of criticism was called in to superintend and direct its operations."[216]

Legouis, though maintaining the Host to be a critic, gives an accurate summary of the Host's concerns in achieving opinions, judgments of the pilgrims. Legouis finds that the Host does not look for metaphors, long words, or eloquence; it is "facts...that matter to him." And whatever "faculties [the Host] may lack, decision is not one of them. He has wide sympathies, and most of the tales he hears gain his approval...[but] he waxes indignant when [a story] relates the misdeeds of a scoundrel."[217] The Host's judgments, then, deal not with literary quality, but with quality of living. The surface Host, that literary critics have tried to recast as one of their own, conceals the figure of Christ as *Judge*.

Turning to the *General Prologue*, we join the group assembled in the Tabard. A highly imaginative setting, it has been called a "poetical microcosm" and likened to "the world." We find, however, that this gathering of some thirty characters housed together is quite an "up-so-doun" world when compared to life as it was actually lived in the 1300s. It is outlandish to have a mixed company of high position and common folk at one inn and "subject to the direction of one man, and that an innkeeper."[218] Remarkable! But more than remarkable, it is an instance of the "signaling" we talked about earlier. This situation could not occur—then why is the poet claiming it did? What does he want us to understand? We need to let the situation nag us; we can't just pass over it. A strong effort is needed to grasp the hidden object.

This active group of participants will spend time "criticising each other's conduct, and delivering their own opinions on religion, morals, [etc.]."[219] Does it seem reasonable that the Franklin, a gentleman land-owner, would really want to know the views of a hired Cook? Would the refined Prioress, a superior in her convent of nuns, wish to spend time in the company of the vulgar Miller? Would the humble Plowman, who does manual labor and transports dung, deem it fitting to sit at table with a distinguished Knight? For such a group to share the evening's accommodations, and travel as companions, is not a daily experience of medieval life; a higher reality is concealed here.

There is an image to be recognized in this inventive allegory, and you need *not* be a fourteenth-century Christian to possess in memory the necessary imagery to draw upon. Where are all persons "equal" and journeying in anticipation of a judgment? This is a way of viewing man's relationship to God. If we take time out from looking for comedy, and watch, instead, for the serious gestures made by Chaucer's words, we will find that the poet, with high motives, really *intended* to present his Host as a domineering lord, an absolute monarch, a pursuer of happiness (that is, the mirth of heaven). It is not ridiculous that the Host dominates; it is His essence; His dedication to bliss, His destiny.

Another element we note is that in the *General Prologue*, the words seem full of life and motion, but we are being deceived. Action, as Baldwin has demonstrated, is a pretense; it is spoken of, not performed. The words move us along from one character to the next, tell of travels in the past, physical appearance, individual reputation, and possible future plans—while the pilgrims themselves stand like colorful cardboard figures allowing the words to play their game, and never spoil the illusion. The first person to move, to speak, to perform, is the Host. The entire *General Prologue* is the build-up for the Host's grand entrance.

Although I am insisting on the importance of the Host in the plan of the *Canterbury Tales*, not everyone has felt his importance. While some recognize him as the center of all the action, others see him as just a facilitator, partly because he tells no tale of his own.[220] In the position of judge, however, a story from his own lips would hardly seem appropriate. And though some have associated an *outline* of Christ with our Host, they hesitated, drew back from complete acknowledgment. But, with clear, Christ-like characteristics, Chaucer creates the Host to be the provider of sustenance and shelter for pilgrims, as well as their guide and judge.

Now let's give a thoughtful look to Chaucer's presentation of the Host, his ultimate character. The Host is the exception in the group, because everyone else is there to begin "implicitly a penitential journey." Chaucer takes a dozen lines to do the groundwork for the entrance. He takes time to describe Christ's manner of speaking; the description gives evidence for future use. Then he recalls that words should be carefully chosen. And, finally, the Host enters with a warm welcome for each pilgrim and immediately provides a fine meal. This identification of the *Host* is the first of sixty-six references to him under that title. Only once, in the introduction to the *Cook's Tale*, will he be called by a personal name (Herry Bailly). If Chaucer "knows" the man's name, why does he choose not to use it? I believe this too is signaling.

Over and over we are bumped and nudged by the word *Host*. Why? What can we make of the word? It was proposed at the outset that *Host* contains "galaxies"; it is an identity of God Himself.

The importance that Chaucer places on just the right word is usually expressed (as here in the *General Prologue*) as "the word must be cousin (closely related) to the *deed*."[221] But Chaucer also writes (in his translation of *Boethius*) that a word must be cousin to the thing of which it speaks. Then as words go, *Host* and *Christ* are closer than cousins. In fourteenth-century doctrine, these words are closer than identical twins.

The word directs our attention to the Host most renowned in the fourteenth century—the Eucharist. The celebration of the Eucharist was (and is) likened to a banquet, a supper, provided for mankind by God. (Poetry, in the previous chapter, spoke of this ceremony as a *feast*, *repast*, etc.) This is precisely the first action of the *Canterbury* adventure. With the introduction of the Host— even before he is described—we see him provide food for his guests.[222]

This *initial* "supper" is spoken of in most excellent, but vague, terms. The meal consists of "victuals (vitaille) of the best" and strong "wine." Examining more intently, the *kind* of food served is not spoken of, nor is the manner of serving. Was it fish, fowl, bread, cheese, soup? Are there many small tables, or several large ones? Can noises be heard from the cooking area? Are there many servers, or few? Is the room warm, well-lighted? Are there pleasant aromas? If the meal is of such fine quality, why aren't we told about it? We are left without specifics—another vaguery.

Because details are omitted, Chaucer allows for the possibility of identifying this "best" food as anything that comes to mind—including the Eucharist. A fourteenth-century lyric that was noted earlier says of the Sacrament, "A better food may no man find."[223] And Chaucer's use of the word *vitaille* (rather than *food*) can be seen as a play on *vital* (living) to indicate Christ as the Living Bread. Hosteler-victualler is a most fitting role description for God; the medieval mind saw Him as provider of all sustenance. Here Chaucer dramatizes this sustainer image.

Following mention of the repast, the narrator offers a seemingly minimal seven-line sketch of the Host. Chaucer presents a notably brief introduction for such an important character, in contrast to those for each pilgrim. It consists of a variety of complimentary statements with a minimum of physical detail. Mainly we find ideas of the atmosphere surrounding the Host and hints of his capabilities, rather than a head-to-toe, recognizable portrait. Each line, however, is dense with significance, each concealing a hidden symbol of Christ:

> A seemly (handsome) man Our Host was withal
> To be a marshal in a hall.
> A large man he was with "stepe" eyes—
> A fairer burgess was there none in Chepe—
> Bold of his speech, and wise, and well-taught,
> And of manhood he lacked nothing.
> And moreover he was right a merry man[224]

Though Chaucer has been accused of skimping on this description, this is only true if you fail to be completely attentive to the words. The first thought is like the *Cursor Mundi* description of Christ, "wonder (wonderfully) seemly [he] was withal."[225]

Chaucer's next line advises that the Host could be a marshal in a hall. Duties of such a marshal are explained in *A Fifteenth-Century Courtesy Book*. They include overseeing meals to be sure everyone has enough, being in charge of those who serve, assigning lodgings, making reckonings, and having the power to correct persons who commit offenses within his jurisdiction.[226] These duties appear very similar to those of the Host; Chaucer's choice of "marshal" is a thoroughly appropriate comparison. But are not these duties also pictured as Christ's functions: to provide sustenance, to be Lord over all men, to say where each will spend eternity, to make reckonings, and to punish (temporally or eternally) those who offend? And the whole phrase, "marshal in a *hall*," holds a greater message.

The poet did not choose the location of a "palace" or a (king's) "court" as the area of his marshal's authority. The "hall" that is overseen could very well be Heaven! Heaven was referred to as "God's hall." *Cursor Mundi* speaks of what "God hath so ordained in his hall." And the MED quotes, "Lord! better is an everlasting day / In thy halls than a thousand; / That is, better is a day in heaven, / Than a thousand here that pass away." The *Exeter Book* says of Christ, "Thou shouldst be head of the noble hall." And in

Ludus Coventriæ the Risen Christ tells Mary Magdalen that He is going to arrange "In heaven a hall for man's sake."[227] Though it is not a description we would use today, Christ as marshal of the hall of Heaven is a properly medieval image.

This marshal is described in the next line as a large man with "stepe" eyes. These eyes are a continuing interpretive problem; connotations of *stepe* take us in many directions; it's difficult to impose a limit. It is as if the word were packed to bursting with possibilities. It can mean "high," "elevated," "large," "prominent," "projecting," "staring," or "wide-open."[228] As a description befitting Christ, one might envision a Judgment portal. In the scene, depicted in the tympanum over a church's western portal, you will often find a large figure of Christ, and his eyes would be elevated—raised to a considerable height above a penitent standing at the doorway. In the style of the time, the eyes would be large, and perhaps protruding. Or, as an alternate impression, we may consider them as the eyes of God, high and elevated looking down from Heaven. As in other cases, all of the above may be intended. But to me, the most appropriate choice is "wide-open."

"Wide-open" is my favorite, because, looking to *Cursor Mundi* once more, we continue the comparison of Christ to a lion that was briefly noted in the previous chapter. Here is another detail from the charming story:

> The lion's whelp, when it is born
> Lies dead until the third morn
> Without life of any limb.
> Then his father comes to him
> And with his roar that is so terrible
> He gives his whelp life to rise.
> So did Jesus our champion
> Though he lay dead for our ransom
> When his Father willed, he made
> Him rise up to gladden us all.
> Of the lion also the nature is he
> Sleeping never closes his eyes
> Nor Jesus, though his ghost he yield.[229]

The Middle Ages believed that lion cubs were stillborn and after three days they awoke when their father roared. Once the cub's eyes were opened, they never closed again; the lion was thought to sleep with his eyes open. It is to be expected (knowing the medieval penchant for relating ideas) that these quaintly incredible characteristics would be compared to Christ's death and resurrection. Christ, like the lion, does not sleep, does not close his eyes. His are "the eyes of the judge that seeth and demeth (judges) all things,"[230] as the final words of Chaucer's *Boethius* relates. These are "stepe" eyes—wide-open always.

And why does Christ not sleep? Because it is He who will "wake us all."[231] Like Christ, the Host accomplishes this task (we will be told) because it is he who breaks the pilgrims' rest so that they may begin their journey to the Heavenly Jerusalem. Chaucer plays out a little scene once again to demonstrate Christ within the Host.

Next, in the narrator's description, we learn that a "fairer burgess" was not to be found in Cheapside. A digression: I want to point out how easily we can slip into "error." Chaucer's line mentions "Chepe," which for most intents and purposes is equivalent to the location "Cheapside," a business district. Use of the longer word seems a trivial difference. But the alteration is important, not at all trivial. To alter *Chepe*, with its many possibilities (the prime example here being *purchase*) is to eliminate its multiple meanings. The traditional expression for Christ's redeeming mankind, as noted earlier, is that He *bought* us. To casually substitute *Cheapside* eliminates the specific image of *purchase* that is projected by "Chepe," the poet's chosen word.

Continuing to examine the same line, "fairer" can refer to being "attractive," or "just" (as in transactions), but it also means "free from moral stain," or "good, virtuous." The line then can be read, "A more virtuous burgess—or, one more free from moral stain— cannot be found in the market (in purchasing)." Only one person surpasses all others in being free from moral stain—Christ. In Chaucer's words, from the mouth of the Parson, "in [Christ] is no imperfection."[232] A purchaser most free of moral stain is our Host, and—on another level of meaning—Christ.

The narrator goes on to tell us that the Host was "bold of his speech, and wise, and well-taught." Many critics appear to disregard this line as they determine that the Host is intellectually lacking. On the contrary, what is conveyed here is that he can handle himself, come what may. We should expect him to speak with authority; his thoughts and decisions, to reflect wisdom; his education, to be superior to most. This training, we can assume, began in his youth because of the allusion to being taught. Compare, then, the description of the young Christ in *Cursor Mundi*. The passage tells how he became separated from his parents at the age of twelve. Mary, his mother, went searching for him.

> Unto the school she [Mary] came
> And a great gathering found therein
> Of wise masters of the law
> Sitting with them she saw Jesus.
> The best masters of that town—
> He gave them all well-prepared reason.[233]

Christ is represented as bold of speech, able to speak freely with the best teachers. He must be wise Himself or these wise teachers would not be impressed with His ability to reason. Once again, the line describing the Host describes the covert image of Christ as well.

The final two lines of the Host's portrait are:

> And of manhood he lacked nothing.
> And moreover he was right a merry man

To say of the Host that he lacked nothing of *manhood* seems redundant, and draws attention because it appears pointless. But the line gains importance from its association with Christ. It takes several pages in *The Lay Folks Catechism* to describe the "seven points of Christ's manhood" setting forth many details of His birth, suffering on the cross, burial, and resurrection "in body and in soul."[234] The purpose of the extensive detail was to discourage heresies that claimed Christ was not to be considered human.

The period (punctuation) that many editors will place following the word *nothing* does not end the sketch, because the next line informs us that he was "right a merry man." Chaucer's "merry" echoes the "Mary" of the doctrine of Christ's birth, which states:

> The first [point of doctrine] is that Jesus Christ, God's
>   Son from heaven
> Was truly conceived of the maiden Mary,
> And took flesh and blood, and became man.[235]

To complete the doctrine of His conception, the *Catechism* continues that Christ became man "through might and strength of the Holy Ghost." Reference to this paternity, by means of the Holy Ghost, appears to be the intent when the Host (twenty-four lines later) alludes to "my father's soul that is dead."[236]

The eleven lines, since the first mention of the Host, delineate a portrait of Christ, beginning with His Eucharistic Presence and ending with the Incarnation. In between the poet touches upon Christ's role in the hall of Heaven, His freedom from sin, His forthrightness and wisdom. In only one line do we learn anything about physical appearance. We are not told about the hands that served the supper, that aided the reckonings. We know nothing of jolly movements while tending his guests. His garb is unmentioned. We know only his grand size and "stepe" eyes. Why? Why only this? Because this bit of physical description can be told without destroying the ambiguity of the portrait.

If particulars of dress, action, face, hair, size and shape of his hands had been put into the image of the Host, it would be the description of just a man, one certain man. Seeing only a large man with prominent eyes, however, allows for a mental image of greater potential. The imagination reviews the words, the pictures; multilayers of information and accumulated details pass before our mind's eye. Some move swiftly, some hesitatingly (as if needing special attention), some move away and then return—awaiting the moment when all will cease their motion, will come to rest as the image of Christ comes into focus. This is the "iconographic dimension" which will "formulate, in a nondiscursive way, [the] truth."[237]

Chaucer's brief sketch (which is, nevertheless, dense with meaning) allows the possibility of Christ peering through the reflections of the Host. Subsequent details will confirm His presence.

Readers of an earlier time, as noted above, recognized Chaucer as expert "in eloquent terms subtle and covert," and would have given the introduction of the Host more than a cursory reading. They would have expected a treasure within; further reading would assure them, and will assure us, of this presence.

The remainder of the *General Prologue* frequently alludes to the "supper," "mirth," and "reckonings," all of which are reminders of Christ's roles concerning pilgrims: sustenance, Heavenly bliss, and the accounting of Judgment. Words and phrases that seem not quite clear as to their intention may refer to a variety of religious thoughts—from Christ's mystical Trinitarian relationship, to man's relationship to God.

The repetition of *mirth* and *bliss* was mentioned earlier as it relates to "signaling." It is inconceivable that Chaucer would compose lines solely to be "monotonous with repetition."[238] We expect his wit and capability to avoid monotony, but *apparent monotony* might serve a special purpose. He pelts his audience with these cheery little words over and over, irritating us to notice. "There is something happening here—notice—notice—notice." Readers are prompted to see, to hear from their memory, thoughts like those recorded in *Ludus Coventriæ*:

> In heaven, to arrange for you a place,
> to my father now will I go
> to mirth and joy and great solace
> And endless bliss to bring you to.[239]

Many have noted this distracting emphasis on the "abiding love of merriness," this "insistence on merriment" which actually "continues throughout the pilgrimage." Baldwin's interest leads him to the NED (later called the OED) and, as a consequence, relates the Host's desire for merriness to medieval quotations of "how merry it would be, to have sight of God's face," and the "mirth of heaven." Delasanta provides Scriptural references to those who are "happy," where "'happy,' of course, is a liturgical neologism for 'blessed.'" Scripture connects this happiness to the anticipated supper: "Blessed is he who shall feast in the kingdom of God." And the newly released soul of Adam (in Coventry's "The Harrowing of

Hell") rejoices, "Now shall we dwell in blissful place / In joy and endless mirth."[240] An aura of bliss mingled with thoughts of the supper to be provided by the Host give indications of Christ to those who would strive for a meaning within.

Baldwin finds the conjunction of cost, reckoning, and mirth notable: "These are strikingly juxtaposed twice: (759-60) and (767-68)."[241] The first instance says that the Host "spoke of mirth among other things / When we had made our reckonings." Here is another Chaucer vaguery: "among other things." The phrase could mean speaking about anything, including Heaven, and the anticipated joy. Baldwin's second example is, "I am thinking of a bit of mirth right now / To give you pleasure, and it shall cost nothing." The joy will cost the pilgrims nothing, because the price had been paid, or in Chaucer's words, "Christ had bought us with His blood." The image of Christ within the Host is bent on bringing joy and will bear the cost, no matter what is asked of Him.

As a matter of fact, the Host makes a remarkable offer though no demands have been made of him: "But be you merry, I will give you my head!"[242] Once again we could pass over the words, sidestep the gesture. But don't you find the words startling? We are supposed to be startled. First, we can see this as a lightly veiled offer of Christ's willingness to die for pilgrims. Consider a second, and equally significant, interpretation of the offer of his head, which is an image of the Mystical Body, a way of meditating upon man's relationship to God. In the Shoreham *Poems* (ca. 1333), we read:

> Christ and His members, men,
> Are one body mystically.[243]

Christ (the Head) and mankind make up this Mystical Body. The Host offering his head to the pilgrims is a Christian tradition, once again dramatized.

Before we continue with the *General Prologue*, let's review the impression Chaucer gives of Doomsday. What will happen? In the words of the Parson, each soul, each pilgrim

owes all his life to God for as long as he has lived, and also for as long as he shall live, [woe unto him] that has no good works to *pay a debt* to God, to whom he *owes* all of his life. For you can trust that "he shall *give accounts*," as St. Bernard says, "of all the good things that have been given him in this present life, and how he has *spent* (or dispensed) them; insomuch that there shall not perish a hair of his head nor a moment of an hour of his time shall perish, that he shall not *give a reckoning* of it."[244]

This vocabulary of Judgment is the vocabulary of the Host's transactions at the close of the *General Prologue*. Here are the debts, the accounts, the spending, the reckoning—and none of it has to do with money, only with God's gifts and judgment.

In the previous chapter, attention was drawn to the ambiguity of the word *auditor*. An auditor is more easily seen as an *examiner* than a *listener*. Chaucer, however, does make the connection between listening and auditing in his *Clerk's Tale*, where we find:

All this shall be done in thy presence;
I will speak nothing out of thine *audience* (hearing).[245]

Auditing, intended as *hearing*, was in Chaucer's thoughts. If we wish to see the surface story as an innkeeper settling accounts, that is reasonable; the covert auditor, however, deals with the *souls*, the consciences, of men, not with their *money*.

Our Host offers a plan for their pleasure, something to make the journey mirthful. And then, strangely enough, requires the pilgrims to agree to this plan—without question or comment—and, stranger still, they do! The Host says:

…therefore I will make some amusement for you,
As I said earlier, and bring you some comfort.
And if you all like, by common consent
To stand at my judgment,
And to perform as I shall tell you,
Tomorrow, when you ride by the way,
    .   .   .
Hold up your hands, without more talk.

And the pilgrims response:

> Our counsel (intention) was not long to seek
> We thought it was not worth deliberation
> And agreed without more reflection,
> We bade him say his verdict as he pleased.[246]

Agreement was quick in coming, though they had not heard the plan. Chaucer's use of "voirdit" (verdict) is remarked upon as too strong for this situation.[247] If so, is this a signal? Are we to take note of how unhesitatingly the pilgrims acquiesced, and how deep was their submission? I think so. We need to react to the problems Chaucer's words create for us. If we say, "You can't really expect to understand everything about this poem," his words cannot perform properly; they need complete audience attention.

If we will allow our mind's eye to randomly scan situations where man finds it necessary to "go along" without demanding, or expecting an explanation in advance, it may not take long to have such a circumstance come into focus. The pattern here is one of deep Christian conviction. The action is universal; it is daily life—man bound to accept each day, though he knows not what lies ahead. When the Host lays out his plan, he expects immediate approval "without more talk." The circumstance dramatizes God's prerogative. Chaucer's Parson gives proper counsel: "Always a man shall put his will subject to the will of God."[248]

It is man's Judge who will demand the reckoning. It is difficult to maintain a serious attitude toward the intentions of the stories when we anticipate that they will instruct and *amuse;* the Middle English phrase says, "tales of best sentence and most solace." *Amusement* is only one equivalent of the medieval word *solace* (solaas). It can say *joy,* and *pleasure,* and also *consolation, comfort, alleviation of sorrow,* and *spiritual joy.* The Pilgrims' tales actually produce many of these qualities—not simply amusement. The limitation indicated by many editors obscures the additional possibilities of Chaucer's line.[249] Instead of allowing "solaas" to show off its complete wardrobe, it has been restricted to wearing only its play clothes.

If we read with Judgment in mind (rather than comedy), we

recognize that "the Host is early characterized as judge whose decrees must be obeyed upon pain of punishment." Then, if judgment is the primary motivation for the *Tales*, seeing the stories as confessions is part of the plan. And, it should follow that, if they are confessions, the tales as "experiences that once happened" are meant to be "memory…[which] recaptures some part of the past."[250] We can expect to hear from the pilgrims' memories. (These memories will be enlarged upon at another time.) They agree to the proposal, saying:

> This thing was granted, our oaths sworn
> With very glad hearts, and prayed [the Host] also
> That he would vouchsafe to do so
> And that he would be our governor
> And judge of our tales.[251]

They gladly took *oaths*—another term too serious for an apparently temporary agreement—and prayed that the Host would be their governor and judge. "Governor" (as in *Cursor Mundi*) traditionally indicates Christ:

> He shall be our Lord and God
> And evermore our governor.

And a medieval poem about the life of Christ proclaims:

> He is our governor forever.

Chaucer himself uses the term related to Christ, as the Man of Law prays, "Now Jesus Christ… / …govern us in his grace." And in Chaucer's translation of *Boethius* he says, "God governs all things in the world…; and that all things will obey (are obliged to) Him." John Lydgate, specifically addressing the Eucharist—the Sacramental Bread—beseeches Christ "in ghostly gladness to govern and guide us." Lydgate's words demonstrate the mind-set of faith.[252]

The pilgrims' acquiescence is of vital importance, their agreement of eternal consequence. We can find a similar scene of instant, unqualified agreement in Exodus 24:3, when "Moses came and told the people all the words of the Lord, and all the judgments: and all the people answered with one voice: We will do all the words of the Lord, which he hath spoken." (Douay-Rheims)

The Host's plan and pilgrims' agreement are overlaid with terms too serious, decisions too automatic; this has been a complaint. But the scene portrays the resignation of profound inevitability—man's inevitable acceptance of God's plan. The weightiness of oaths and verdicts indicates a signal to Chaucer's audience,[253] an indication that there is more bound up in these words than mere friendly plans.

The pilgrims, when they readily accepted the Host as their judge, asked him to be their governor, and indicated one more task as well, to be their reporter. Christ, in the Chester play of the *Last Judgment*, is addressed as the "Lord of lords, King of kings, / and *Informer* of all things," and the *Grail Legend* portrays a sinner asking Christ to have pity and mercy "my sins to *report*." The information gathered must have a recipient; there must be a destination for the reports. The receiver of these reports—the Judgments Christ makes of sins, of confessions—will be God the Father. We are told in Cynewulf's *Last Judgment* that men will come before "God's Son" and "*the Father*...will *learn* / how...[men] have guarded their souls" while on earth. And in the Wyclif Gospel of John, Jesus asks if men expect him *to accuse them* before God the Father. The "advocate with the Father [is] Jesus Christ," the Epistle 1John tells us, and Mirk presents Christ as our true and eternal advocate. A powerful recommendation from the dying Christ was, "Father, forgive them, they know not what they do." With an implied presence of the Father, we now have reviewed all of the Trinity in the *General Prologue*. The third person of the Trinity (the Holy Ghost) had played a part earlier, when the Host called upon "my father's soul that is dead." Having the entire Trinity introduced in this opening scene at the Tabard lends a new possibility to those who will cover the expense of the "supper at all *our* cost."[254]

The Host's speaking of "all *our* cost" (the cost of us all) comes before he had confided his intention to be part of the group of travelers. "Our" can be read as an imperial form, such as a king declaring "it is *our* decision that..." or God the Father's proclamation seen earlier (in the *Annunciation Play*), "Righteousness will *we* perform." The inclusion of "all," allows us to see the "cost," on the level of hidden meaning, belonging to the Trinity,[255] rather than to the pilgrims, as we might otherwise suppose. This anticipated supper (which can be interpreted as the Heavenly Banquet) at the end of the pilgrimage, the Host declares, will be at "our" cost—the Father, Son, and Holy Ghost. Notably, the form is reminiscent of Genesis 1:26 in the Creation story. In the account of Creation, the days are progressing as God says, "Let there be a firmament... Let the waters bring forth... Let the earth bring forth..." But when God comes to the creation of man, He says, "Let *us* make man to *our* image and likeness." (Douay-Rheims) It is "We," the Trinity, who will preside over the supper at the end of man's life. This is "our" banquet for which the Host will "set a certain price," a nebulous statement in the surface interpretation (and again no mention of *money*), but the concealed sentence intends the price as the redemptive act of Christ, the promised action of the Trinity: Father, Son, and Holy Ghost.[256]

This body of pilgrims, we hear, will "go by the *way*," and a few lines later Chaucer refers to "ride by the *way*." Robinson speculates that this *way* may intend the Canterbury Road, as we would presume in the surface context. In the underlying sentence, the covert religious sense, the "Way" is a referent to the Christian religion (in Acts of the Apostles) as well as the concept of pilgrimage, both literal and figurative. And we recall that St. Augustine used similar wording—"all men joined to Christ by faith and love are 'on the way.'"[257] In much of the vocabulary chosen by the poet, it is not difficult to find a religious reflection just beneath the surface.

It has been noted that the Host is the exception in the Canterbury group; he is the only one *not* dedicated to the journey by the pledge of pilgrimage. He tells them he will ride with them and freely dedicates himself to be their guide. It is difficult to ignore the basic image presented to our mind's eye. Chaucer, on four occasions, calls upon God as *guide* of mankind, and in three other places he indicates that it is God who *leads* men.[258] The Host's offer provides another enduring Christian image. (The imagery is current today. Pope John Paul II closed his homily at a worldwide celebration of the Eucharist in 1989 with the declaration that can be seen to parallel the central idea of Chaucer's plan: "[It is] our Saviour, whose presence in the Eucharist accompanies us on our earthly pilgrimage!"[259])

Our remaining considerations in the *General Prologue*, for the time being, involve the Corpus Christi ceremonies. (The basis of this celebration is of the utmost importance because its main purpose is to draw attention to the Consecrated Host, the Bread of the Altar. No matter what *day*, or occasion, was chosen for the event, the basis for celebrating was thanksgiving for the existence of the Host.[260]) The first thread of a connection comes from Chaucer's Host himself: "For truly, there is no comfort or mirth, / To ride by the way *dumb as a stone*." He is about to suggest the telling of tales. Hardin Craig, in *English Religious Drama of the Middle Ages*, remarks that:

> it has been suggested that the Corpus Christi plays began as *dumb-show* pageants in the procession and developed gradually from dumb show into drama as the procession moved along.[261]

It is as if Chaucer is confirming by experience (or had heard about) the developmental process of the "ancient custom" of the drama which Craig describes. It is a dull ride "dumb as a stone"; the Host wants something better, livelier. It seems that performances are called for. As the feast day dramas came to be, so will the tales of the pilgrims.

Now we watch the early-morning happenings in the Tabard. The night has passed. Soon the group will be ready to begin its journey. The narrator tells us:

> In the morning, when the day began to spring,
> Up rose our Host, and was our cock,
> And gathered us together all in a flock,
> And forth we rode at a little more than walking-pace (paas)
> To the watering of St. Thomas;
> And there our Host...stopped his horse.[262]

At the break of day the Host rose and gathered his flock. They rode slowly—at little more than walking-pace—and are associated with water (somehow related to St. Thomas), and they stop. This has all the indications of a symbolic event, rather than an attempt at reality.

We hear (see) nothing of preparations—no breakfast, no transport of possessions, no saddling of horses, no sounds or movements, no mention of weather, nor attitudes of the pilgrims. Who was the first one ready? Who caused a delay? Did they ride two by two, or single file, or as a close group through the streets? If they rode horses, why did they move so slowly (at a walking-pace) perhaps as far as two miles before halting? The leisurely beginning could be the reason they will be pressed for time at the end of the journey.

What we have here, instead of the reality of setting out upon a pilgrimage, can be seen as a parallel to the description of a Corpus Christi procession. It is early in the day and the Eucharist (the Host), reverently displayed, is raised up for all to see. (The priest's elevating of the Host during the Mass became identified with the Consecration, the moment when the bread became Christ.[263]) The worshipers—traditionally dignitaries, clergy, religious, guildsmen and others (as are the pilgrims)—join in procession. Ceremonial processions, mentioned earlier, would travel precisely at a walking-pace, until they arrived at their first station, which was often a water conduit. Conduits, raised stage-like structures, were the accepted focal points for ceremonies or performances. The conduit in Cheapside is of particular importance to us, because it was near "one of the most celebrated religious institutions in London, the Hospital of St. Thomas."[264] So this prominent landmark could be the source of Chaucer's inspiration for a water supply named for St. Thomas.

Because of Chaucer's skill and ingenuity with multifaceted images, it is also worth our pausing to consider the word chosen by the poet. He selects *watering*, not *water*. A watering is not only a *place* (for water), but it can be an *action*, to pour, soak with, or immerse in water.

A water source as a *place* could be the conduit already mentioned. It could also be the site of the usual reading given us by researchers into actual locations on the London-to-Canterbury road.

This *water of St. Thomas*, we learn from Skeat, was a watering place for horses at the two-mile marker.[265] The group was traveling at a leisurely pace. It would hardly be necessary to water fresh horses after only two miles; there is never another mention of watering the horses or caring for them in any way. The significance of indicating this water seems more important for mentioning the water itself than in caring for horses. And specifying a water source provides the opportunity to use the name of St. Thomas; I have found Chaucer's inclusion of names always meaningful. But, however we would speculate, in addition to the ceremonies at a water conduit near St. Thomas Hospital, we can now see horses slaking their thirst at St. Thomas stream.

And, as an *action* of watering, we turn to the biblical sense of water—that which "satisfies spiritual needs." (A fifteenth-century prayer book was called *The Conduit of Comfort* because "the water thereof refreshed the soul."[266]) *Prayer*, such as the Corpus Christi liturgy of Aquinas, is another view of "watering of St. Thomas." Then the lines would be saying, "They proceeded slowly surrounded by the prayers of St. Thomas (Aquinas)." As they make their way, the Latin liturgy is being intoned.

Now to collect our possibilities. Chaucer, of course, used the word *stream* in his poetry. He also used the word *conduit* on two occasions. Both of these—stream and conduit—could have been chosen, but the all-inclusive *water* was the poet's choice as the group pauses. Which image is intended? We can see the literal group of riders on horseback, or an alternate image of a procession on foot, or the intangible (spiritual) edification of being immersed in the prayers of Aquinas. (His *Lauda, Syon*, considered a perfect liturgical chant, was often used in processions.[267]) Chaucer would not have found it hard to be clear in such a description, had he wished, but he chose no clear image. This appears to be one of the poet's purposeful *vagueries*. As Kolve has shown—ambiguity is the answer.

The line could have been simple, if he had wanted it to be. Instead, his poem tosses out an innocent-looking phrase—"the watering of St. Thomas"—and, if we try to grasp it, we are amazed at its weight. Then, with fluid ease, we find we now have triplets of interpretation from "the watering." We can't be expected to choose between three newborns; we will not let go of any of them until we know which of them (perhaps each of them) is part of the diverging lifeline of the poem.[268]

We are ready to move to a different vantage point to take a second look at two of the lines we have dealt with previously. Before we do that, it goes without saying that today, if we speak of "not using the Lord's Name in vain," there are many who would think this old-fashioned, or superstitious—or perhaps be unaware of what is meant. Not so in centuries past. Terms such as "by golly," "by gosh," and "by gum" are remnants of a time when God's Name in conversation was never heard. These, and many other forms (like *Egad* and *Gadzooks*), were distorted pronunciations "from a desire to avoid actual use of the sacred name." One of the earliest such forms was *cock*, intending "a veiled variant of God." It was used in medieval exclamations, such as "by cock" (by God!), "for cock's pain" (for God's pain!), "by cock's soul" (by God's soul!). You'd even find the expression in medieval plays. For example, a scolding Caiaphas, angered over a delay in the Crucifixion, blurts out, "For Cock's face!"[269] Chaucer, too, uses "For cock's bones!" twice in the *Canterbury Tales*. Although it sounds strange to us, we need to attune our mind's ear to accept *cock* as a substitute for the word *God*.

Keeping this substitution in mind, let's look at the early morning scene at the Tabard once more. Chaucer's lines are,

> Up rose our Host, and was our cock,
> And gathered us together all in a flock

If Chaucer's use of *cock* in the first line is a purposeful substitute for *God*, and we exchange the word in question, the result is, "Up rose our Host, and was our God / And gathered us together all in a flock." This can be seen as the Elevation of the Bread (our Host) becomes Christ (our God) before a congregation gathered to celebrate the presence of the Eucharist as God's gift to mankind. When Christians (such as these Pilgrims) are referred to as a flock, it is *understood* that Christ is their Shepherd.[270] The poet himself speaks of Christ as mankind's shepherd in the *Second Nun's Tale*. Though the word *shepherd* is never mentioned in the *General Pro-*

logue, it would have been recognized in the dramatizing, and would have produced the proper mental image. We see, once again, an epithet (the Good Shepherd) in performance. These lines also conceal an expression of faith in the dogma of Transubstantiation: the Host is our God (our cock). And when dealing with Chaucer's words, turnabout is fair play; this expression of faith also confirms Christ's presence within Chaucer's Host and Guide of the pilgrims.

We have watched the pilgrims moving slowly "to the watering of Saint Thomas" where the Host stops his horse; this too provides a devout underlying image. Christ was often compared to a champion Knight, and his "horse" was the Cross of His Crucifixion, as we learned earlier. Miri Rubin tells of a mid-fourteenth-century sermon that holds an interesting relationship to the scene we are reviewing. The sermon was composed for Corpus Christi and contains "vibrant references to tale and allegory." It speaks of Christ on His journey to Heaven, the allegory paralleling the action of our Host setting forth from the Tabard. An honored man mounts a horse; this action replicates that of the priest at Consecration as he "raise[s] Christ aloft in his hands." The equestrian ride is then compared to the exposition of the Eucharistic Host carried in procession.[271] As we have noted before, the underlying images of Christ to be seen in Chaucer's words are often the expression of a medieval thought pattern; they are not necessarily an unprecedented inspiration for the *Canterbury Tales* alone.

Processional images underlie the surface description which has dominated attention for more than a century. The skillful introduction of the Host concealed a series of covert images dealing with Christ's Judgment, as well as a celebration of the Eucharist and an affirmation of dogmas subtly expressed for those who would search for them. Of all the possibilities that we have considered—significant words, actions, and relationships of the Host in the *General Prologue*—none would have been possible if Chaucer had introduced this character by his "given" name. The mirth of a man named "Herry" would be nothing more than mirth; the judgment of the stories would only involve their value as stories; and the Corpus Christi images just noted would never have existed. The guide of the pilgrims is the ever-present Host, a covert identity hidden (as Boccaccio said) so "the ultimate discovery...shall be more precious."

The adventure that is just beginning holds commonplace images of the road of life, the journey from birth to death, from earth to the Celestial City. And Chaucer acknowledged that it was God's province to lead mankind. Images encompass "where two or three are gathered in My name, I am with them." The Host's offer to guide the group is an offer also identified at Towneley with Christ, "I shall go before, / That your going I may guide."[272]

One of the loveliest petitions for God's help on life's journey comes from the words of the well-known *Panis Angelicus*, another hymn for Corpus Christi:

> We ask You, Godhead, three in one,
> to come to us even as we worship You.
> Guide us along Your paths
> to our journey's end.[273]

The journey's end for Chaucer's pilgrims is Canterbury Cathedral.

Cathedrals, it is understood, are identified with the City of God, but Canterbury has an even more specialized identity. Construction of the cathedral was begun many centuries before Chaucer lived, and dedicated then to "Christ Jesus the Saviour." It is "the mother church of England." Called the *Cathedral of Christchurch*, "no mortal folk could claim it as their home in quite the way in which it was Christ's." Knowing this about the destination makes this truly the journey of Christ leading pilgrims to their celestial home. The word *Canterbury* leads a double life, then, with both tangible and spiritual meanings; not only is it the earthbound cathedral to medieval men, but it was "the Heavenly Jerusalem," understood by all to be "the House of God" upon earth.[274] It is the pilgrim Parson's announced intention to show the way of the "glorious pilgrimage to the heavenly Jerusalem." This journey to Canterbury, which provides no arrangements for meals or sleep, can be seen as the "road to eternity," and therefore is not intended "as a place for rest or sleep, but rather to be traveled...since any pilgrimage is of its essence a rehearsal for death and judgment."[275]

We are about to leave the *General Prologue*. There is more to learn about our Host as he deals with those he is guiding. When we have considered a number of his interactions, and have acquired more of an understanding of what Chaucer is about, we will make a return visit to the Tabard in the *General Prologue*. For now, let's begin our journey.

Once under way, the pilgrims deliver the confessional stories as requested by the Host. In the course of several of the entr'actes, the interludes of conversation joining many of these little dramas, more information about the Host is disclosed. (Lumiansky has serendipitously called these interludes "a movable stage," which reflects the means often used to progress from one story to the next in the day-long performances of the *Corpus Christi* plays.[276])

Throughout several of these connecting passages, we hear the Host utter his supposedly objectionable language. What is it that is objectionable? What do his oaths amount to? Nine are direct references to Christ's passion and death, for example, "for God's worshipful passion"; and "By the cross that St. Helen found."[277] In the previous chapter, we learned how the "oaths" scattered throughout *The Second Shepherd's Play* were used as a "reliving" of Christ's life, and a means of involving the medieval audience. In the *Canterbury Tales*, oaths may have the same purpose. For the Christic identity within the Host, these are personal recollections; for pilgrims (and Chaucer's audience), they are reminders of Christ's role in salvation. If the Host's oaths refer to Christ's Passion from the point of view of the third person, we have learned that that does not disqualify the speaker from being Christ; it was an accepted convention used by fourteenth-century poets and dramatists.

What about the oaths that do not involve Christ's Passion? Fifteen are simple references, requesting "God's mercy," or saying "God bless you," and such. Four expressions address holy figures, "By St. Augustine!" for example, or they mention faith or salvation—all are natural things for Christ to say.[278] If we simply take them seriously, such thoughts are what we would expect from Christ.

But what about the curses? There are two: "Tell on, the Devil's way" and "God give you sorrow."[279] The first of these curses is directed at the Miller who is drunk. The second calls down sorrow upon the Cook, who also appears drunk. Do curses denote criticism toward the actions of these characters? It seems likely. But, in the end, we need only remember that homilists justified God's cursing and swearing, and the Miller and Cook are surely not to be *blessed* for their behavior.

Two other expletives are unique: "Dun (presumably the name of a horse) is in the mire!" and "Straw for your high-breeding (or *nobility*)!"[280] They don't appear to be offensive, and their lively images cause me to suspect that they hold a very special meaning related to the circumstances of their occurrence. Unfortunately, the words have eluded attempts to grasp them; their special meaning has not yet been surrendered.

A final consideration of the Host's colorful language is a most meaningful expression, although it is regularly treated otherwise. Particular attention needs to be paid to this exclamation from the Host: "'Harrow!' said he, 'by nails and by blood!'" "Harrow," Baugh explains, is "a common ejaculation, of obscure origin." In this case, however, followed by "nails and blood" it produces the scene of man's salvation. Interrupting the continuity of the expression with "said he" makes the association less obvious. Removing the interruption we have, "Harrow, by nails and by blood." Did we talk enough about the Harrowing of Hell and the fourteenth century? Does it evoke a response in *your* memory as it might for Chaucer's contemporaries? We hear a recollection of the harrowing of hell, as a consequence of being crucified. The memory of hell, and the force exerted against evil is the Host's response to a "false churl and false justice" from *The Physician's Tale*. This "harrow" is not obscure at all; it is the object of Christ's sacrifice. He came to harrow hell, to "burst the strong brass gates / And steel locks that thereon hung / ... / Then they should be merry and glad, / The folks that were in woeful state."[281]

If we peer beneath the surface meaning, and look to covert possibilities, the Host as Christ is speaking, chiding, remembering as we would expect. He asserts his authority; he reproaches the wicked; he alludes to his part in the plan of Salvation. For those who would find blasphemy in the Host's words, we need only consider that God himself *could not* use God's name in vain, nor could He blaspheme.

Though the Host's expletives are regularly assumed to be

offensive, in fairness now, let's give particular attention to his con-
ciliatory outbursts, his calls for "peace." As the Friar and Sum-
moner argue at the end of the *Wife of Bath's Prologue*, the Host
cries out for "Peace! and that at once!" so that the Wife may begin
her tale. When her story is concluded, the Friar resumes goading
the Summoner. And again the Host calls, "Peace, no more of this!"
Now the Friar begins a story, but he is interrupted by the Sum-
moner, and for the third time we hear the Host's call for "Peace."
When the Friar repays the Summoner by interrupting as the Sum-
moner tells his story, the Host steps in yet again calling for
"Peace."[282]

The situation is a testy one. But of all the variety of words that
Chaucer could have put into the mouth of the Host—silence, stop,
hold your tongue, close your mouth—four times his choice is *peace*.
The other words I've suggested were not used by the poet because
they would not enhance the developing image of the Host's char-
acter; they do not fit the process that is unfolding. The repetition is
a signal once again, to attract attention to the Host. The words are
saying, "See this man as the 'bringer of peace.'" Christ, in the
Epistles, is called "God of Peace," and "Lord of Peace," and in me-
dieval plays declares himself "the true Prince of Peace."[283] In creat-
ing hostility between the Friar and the Summoner, the poet begets
the proper circumstance to act out one more medieval epithet, to
trigger a medieval sign—Lord of Peace.

In another interlude, the *Prologue to the Nun's Priest's Tale*, we
can detect an allusion to the Real Presence (of Christ in the Sacra-
ment of the Altar). As this Prologue begins, the Monk has just had
his story of "tragedies" interrupted. After a few lines, the Host ad-
dresses the Monk, and then goes on to say:

> For certainly, as these clerics say,
> Whereas a man may have no audience,
> It helps nothing to tell his sentence (meaning, teaching,
>   doctrine).
> And well I know the substance is in me,
> If anything shall well-reported be.[284]

This is one of Chaucer's tantalizing, troublesome sections. Baugh presumes that the line about "substance" intends, "I have the capacity to understand," but the idea is not clearly stated. Instead of subscribing to Baugh's reading, which may be acceptable for the surface story, we will allow "substance" to give its mystical performance, to impress us with its honors gained from associating with theologians. The Host confides that clerics tell us that if you have no audience, it doesn't help to present a message. This sounds like an "alert," a line to arouse attention—if no one is listening, there is no point in giving a message.

What immediately follows is, "Well I know that the substance is in me—if anything shall well-reported be." The Host alerts his audience and then states that the substance is in him. "Substance," here, is the crucial word; like *pilgrimage* and *crusade*, it is steeped in the chalice of the Middle Ages. *Substance*, the primary definition in the OED says: "Essential nature, essence; *esp. Theol.*, with regard to the being of God, the divine nature or essence." The entry quotes the Athanasian Creed (1325) regarding Christ, "He is God, of the *substance* of the Father begotten before the world [began]." And in *Boethius*, Chaucer states "goodness is the *substance* of God and of blissfulness." In addition, the first entry in the MED says *substance* is "used of the incarnate Christ."[285] The word is saturated with the spirit of medieval faith.

This declaration of *substance* being within the Host is also the confirming of Tran*substantia*tion. Lesson V from the Divine Office for Corpus Christi says: "In [this sacrament] bread and wine are changed *substantia*lly into the body and blood of Christ." The Eucharistic Host, in the vocabulary of Scholastic Theology, is described as the "accidents" (the attributes or qualities) of bread that can be seen, while the "substance" (or essence) mystically becomes the body of Christ.[286] As a parallel, Chaucer's imaginative allegory describes the accidents, the attributes of the Host (Herry Bailly) that can be seen; these overt qualities conceal the substance, the Presence of Christ. Chaucer's Host is indicating his covert identity, and wants this fact well reported by alerting that audience who would recognize that the poet is "telling his sentence" (doctrine, hidden meaning).

The Host's given name, which I've mentioned several times, makes its single appearance in the link to the *Cook's Tale*. The Host calls the Cook by name, "Roger," and the Cook, in turn, refers to the Host with:

Herry Bailly, by thy faith[287]

There is no reaction to the name being revealed; it never appears again. Then why bother? Why not fill out the line with other information? What purpose could the poet have for using it, for creating it, except as another signal? Otherwise the mention appears to serve no purpose. The significance of this name, however, conceals a whole world—no, a *universe*—of information. What a task for these two little words!

To begin, this name is doubly rare because the Host is the only person who is twice blessed, the only traveler in the *Tales* who is identified by two names. There must be a good reason for each. One well-documented reason for choosing this name must be that a living person, an innkeeper, in fourteenth-century London had a similar name: Henri Bayliff (*Henricus Bailiff*, in the document discovered).[288] It seems curious to me that the Host is called an *innkeeper* by many writers, but Chaucer *never* claims that he is. (There is an "insignificant" difference between an *inn* and a *hostel*.) Have we been so confounded with the finding of this "real" Henri Bayliff, innkeeper, that we have confidently adopted his identity for the Host? Have we been gulled? Ought we murmur, in chorus, *mea culpa*? Absolutely not. I believe Chaucer planned to confuse the identities. How better to hide his covert intention than by giving a distracting outward appearance of reality?

As Delasanta says, Chaucer uses "decoying realism" to throw his pursuers "off the scent." This name that Chaucer bestows on the Host is slightly different from that of the contemporary innkeeper. We asked in an earlier situation, "Why the slight change?" Chaucer's spelling is *Herry* (not Henri) Bailly. Though his name adds one more detail to the image, the ever-present identity remains *the Host*, allowing a more complex identity than only that of a real man who once lived in London.

We will ask the poem to offer just one word, one name at a time; both together would be too unwieldy. Let's make note, at the outset, that each *name* wears a capital letter as a mask; when not masked, each is an ordinary Middle English word.

Remembering that spelling in the Middle Ages was creative, flexible, we will make our start with *Herry* as "herie." The word can mean, "to praise...to worship." Examples in fourteenth-century poetry are numerous: "Holy Father, I herie Thee"; "All that is in heaven Thee herieth"; "O God, the high Trinity / All souls herie Thee." Chaucer, too, gives us examples: "God they thank and herie" and "[He] herieth Christ, who is King of Heaven."[289] Our poet, by choosing this name for the Host, also "herieth" Christ!

There is more. The verb *harry* (harrow) in the OED is defined, "to despoil *hell;* as said of Jesus Christ after his death." The entry cites *Cursor Mundi,* "Our Lord *heried* (harrowed) hell." The MED lists *harie,* "hostile action," or *heri,* "to rob (hell)." *Lay Folks Catechism* says, "the Godhead went unto hell, And *heried* (harrowed) it." The *Gospel of Nicodemus* talks of prophecies of "how [Christ] should *herie* (harrow) hell." Even Chaucer's Miller refers to Christ as "Him that *heried* hell."[290]

One more variation will complete the present possibilities for the first name. If *Herald* is also implied in "Herry," it is proper and fitting because (as the MED helps us to understand) a herald would make announcements, introduce people, report actions, and award prizes.[291] This is the Host's role in a nutshell! What a relief this little word must feel, to finally be delivered of its burgeoning possibilities.

And what of "Bailly?" Where does it lead? First, a *bailly* is a position held by someone whose authority has been delegated by a superior; a bailly is the administrator of an area. But *bailly* is also a way of referring to a place, a district (or bailiwick) of guardianship. Of Adam (before the Fall), it is said that "God gave him a mastery (or dominance)...of paradise, the bailly (the administrator)." In another setting, we hear the first Torturer in the Towneley play of the *Scourging* say to Jesus, "Thou art here in our bailly (district)." Elsewhere Jesus taunts Satan with, "In that bailly shall you ever be, / Where sundry sorrows never cease."[292] The association of *bailly* and *bailiwick* add the eschatalogical sense, a favorite phrase for warning of Judgment being "give an account of your Baily-wick." All these "accidents" of identification veil the Presence of Christ.

As we grasp these two humble words it seems almost overwhelming to try to embrace all they contain: a herald from heaven; a bailly to be worshiped; the authority figure, who is reporter of actions and awarder of prizes; the vanquisher of hell (*hell* being the devil's bailly). The name that Chaucer provides for his Host touches the whole universe—from celestial realms, to earthly domains, to infernal regions. Time and eternity merge, within "Herry Bailly"—our Host. Once again we see Chaucer's phenomenal skill, his ability to find words that are cousins to what he wishes to express.[293]

Leaving the bailey who is "heried," we proceed through the *Tales* and stop to look at the Host's encounter, better yet confrontation, with the Pardoner. (By his title, we know this traveler's importance involves giving pardon.) Much has been made of this scene, because the Pardoner (a clergyman) appears to reveal embarrassing information about the Host. The Pardoner is offering to absolve each pilgrim of his or her sins. As he finishes promoting this cause, he turns to the Host saying:

> I advise that our Host here shall begin
> For he is most enveloped in sin.[294]

Enveloped is a slippery word and no doubt carefully chosen. We need to use care not to let it slip past us without allowing us to examine its intentions. The Pardoner is not addressing a sinful man, that is, a sin-*filled* man. Our slippery word indicates that sins are *external* to the Host, sin surrounds, envelops the Host. The image we should be seeing was noted in *The Harrowing of Hell*, where Christ replies to Satan's threats:

> Sin found thou never
> *In* Me as in other men.[295]

When men, "like sheep have gone astray...the Lord hath laid on him the iniquity of us all." It is the Savior, as Chaucer's Parson tells us, "Jesus Christ [who] took upon Himself the pain of all our wickednesses," but "*in* Him is no imperfection." Sin is closely associated with Christ, but it is external to His being; it envelops Him—as it does our Host.

We have spoken of the Host's words, mainly his outbursts, that have been found harsh and sometimes confusing to the reader. But there is no doubt that the most confusing phrases he utters are found in his unique style of Latin. We can not attribute improper forms to author-ignorance, because the educated man in the fourteenth century was expected to know Latin. We should not write it off as the Host's ignorance either, because in his portrait in the *General Prologue* we are specifically told that he was well-taught. But here we are, once again, stopped by the Host's speech. Chaucer seems to enjoy hiding information in the words he puts into the mouth of the Host. It is only to be expected that more than surface meaning would come from the words of Christ, and so this is as it should be.

Chaucer sees to it that our Host has many ways of attracting attention by his verbal expressions, including his peculiar Latin constructions. Be assured that it is not necessary to actually be able to read Latin to understand the problem. It only concerns three words: *corpus* (body), *Dominus* (Lord), and *bones* (to be explained shortly). Scholarly writers who know Latin give us all the information we need, in order to comprehend where the trouble lies.

I think most people know that words in Latin have different endings—a word comes with a supply of different hats to wear, depending on the occasion. *Dominus* is different from *domini,* is different from *dominum*, etc. (It's rather like *me, myself,* and *I;* it's all the same person spoken of, but each word means something slightly different.)

A nineteenth-century Latin scholar, Walter Skeat, in his notes for the *Prioress' Prologue*, gives us the typical comment about these Latin phrases: "*corpus dominus;* of course for *corpus domini,* the Lord's body. But it is unnecessary to correct the Host's Latin."[296] (The idea is that the Host is being taken as foolish or as a show-off, so we don't need to make corrections.) And later, in the conversation that joins *The Physician's Tale* with *The Pardoner's Tale,* the Host exclaims "*corpus bones.*" Skeat finds this "form of oath is amusingly ignorant" and feels that the Host "evidently regards *corpus* as a genitive case." But what if Chaucer has something entirely different in mind?

It isn't ignorance of Latin on the part of Chaucer that produces these unorthodox combinations; ingenuity is a better guess than ignorance. Though no one had ever assigned these words to join in tandem before, Chaucer saw their capabilities and had confidence in their resourcefulness. It's up to us to find the means of helping them keep faith in their singular task. It might be that these combinations are a way of dramatizing the medieval denouncement of Christ's speech, as noted by Wyclif. In one of his Sermons, the preacher complains that "words of Christ are scorned by grammarians."[297] The Host might be acting out the opinion of the day by using "faulty" constructions. But my guess is that it's really much more involved, gives us much more to think about than incorrect grammar.

Unique grammar is a better bet. After all, if this is God (Christ) talking about His own body, who can say which are the proper endings for *Him* to use? So, if Chaucer is thinking about how to express this, the poet's inventiveness might have provided the answer: use only the nominative case. With nominative endings, we have *Dominus, Corpus,* and *Bones*—that is, *the Good. Bones* can be explained now, not as the plural of the English word *bone,* but as the equivalent of *Good* intended as the term for God as Absolute Good.[298] The pairs of Latin words, then, can be seen as appositives. There are examples of this in the *Office of Corpus Christi: Christus Dominus, Dominus Deus, Dominus Iesus*—meaning Christ, the Lord; the Lord God; Lord Jesus, respectively. What Chaucer's words could be saying then is "the Body, God Himself" and "the Body, Goodness Itself." In choosing *the Good,* in this way, it is similar to Chaucer's statement elsewhere (also beginning with an appositive), "God Himself is sovereign good."[299]

The point is, that however we choose to explain these unique Latin expressions, these words act as obtrusive references, they are signals, directing our attention to the Eucharist: God's Body, the Eucharistic Host. Those who expect a hidden message see them as the Host flaunting his covert identity—Christ Himself.

Now, as we draw near to the end of our considerations, the elements needing examination become more deeply medieval, where the understanding of the intention has been lost to us. We must leave behind the twentieth century with its scientific advances and its skepticism in matters of faith. Our thinking, our imagination will need assistance from medieval sources to try to bring into focus what may now be completely alien to our mind's eye. The points to be covered are the Host's concern over the setting sun, his apparent change of plan regarding the number of stories to be told, the medieval impression of time, what was understood by *pilgrimage*, and the function of the Tabard. At times these topics, of necessity, interconnect and influence each other.

We will begin with the Host's involvement with time. His ability to calculate the time of day "by means of sun and shadow" is noteworthy, along with his directives to employ time responsibly. He is concerned as the day comes to an end. When one reviewer asks, "What...is the rush?" and attributes "sheer impatience and fear of boredom" as the Host's motivation, we find today's frustrations engulfing this fourteenth-century figure. Delasanta, reassuringly, puts us back into Chaucer's time by affirming that "the Host urges his charges to eschatological haste before the sun sets."[300] Chaucer's Parson, who is commissioned to tell the final story, warns against the "misspending of time" and confirms an appropriate reason for urgency as he exhorts the pilgrims with the words of St. Bernard, "Man shall give account of everything he has been given...not a moment of an hour shall be lost, that he will not have to reckon for."[301] Time is precious; we must not waste a moment in idleness. The message is, "The end is near."

But if the end is near, what about the "return" journey? The Host complicates our new dilemma with what appears to be a change of plan regarding the stories he had requested. Let's review the Host's original proposal about the elaborate sequence of stories to be told.

...I pray you...

. . .

> That each of you, to shorten the way,
> On this journey, shall tell two tales
> Toward Canterbury, I mean it so,
> And homeward he shall tell another two.[302]

That sounds as if four are required from each pilgrim. But then, in the *Parson's Prologue* (the introduction to the last story), after only twenty-one of the twenty-nine pilgrims have been heard from (plus the Canon's Yeoman, a tag along), the Host declares:

> ...Lords (masters) everyone,
> Now we lack no more tales than one
> Fulfilled is my sentence and my decree.[303]

This doesn't say that he has changed his plan; he says the "decree" has been accomplished! It appears to be a "direct contradiction" and an abandonment of the original plan, in spite of the fact that the "pilgrims bound themselves *by oath*." It certainly looks like another signal. A signal category we hadn't employed before has to do with "some seeming mistake...[or] an apparent *non sequitur*" which catches the attention. It surely seems to apply here. Many have tried to explain or excuse this serious lapse of memory (or determination) on the part of Chaucer, or his Host. Is it possible that what appears to be a contradiction is, instead, two equivalent views of the plan? There must be something we are missing.

Let's examine the "contradiction." First, if we take Chaucer at his word, that only one more tale needs to be told, at least three things come to mind simultaneously. First, some of the pilgrims have never said a word. Secondly, Pilgrim Chaucer is the only journeyer who actually told two tales (one was interrupted, the other completed). And, finally, there will be *no* tales told on the "homeward" journey, so what happens to the Host's original intention to bring comfort and mirth, and avoid a "ride by the way dumb as a stone?" Is this a change of personality, and plan, as well as a change in the author's intention? We'll pursue this further.

But first we'll approach our dilemma from a different angle. Part of our problem is a lack of understanding of the medieval sense of time. A digression is needed. Our usual linear feeling toward time (coming from somewhere before dinosaurs, existing today, and stretching on into the twenty-first century and beyond) needs to be put on hold. For the moment, put yourself back in England late in the autumn of 1385: no advantages of alternate use of central heating and air conditioning to keep our private world perfect; no thermal underwear or galoshes; no electric lights or electric blankets.

As this medieval winter wears on, the landscape becomes various tones of black, gray, and white. Much of each room, in every kind of shelter, is bitterly cold and dim. The food supply has little variety; fruits and vegetables dwindle to non-existence. And then—a warm breeze, a tree with leaves budding, the song of a bird—spring has returned. Life is renewed. All nature blesses you, and the promise of a season of comfort and plenty brings rejoicing (even with the knowledge that the gray and cold will return). It is difficult for us, with all our creature comforts, to picture the intensity of hardship and deprivation when Chaucer lived—the trial of getting through another winter—and the unrestrained joy of spring's return. People were very conscious of time and the change of seasons. They were closely attuned to the cycles of animal life: the birthing of spring lambs, the time for bees to swarm and birds to nest.[304]

If you have tried to gain a feeling of being immersed in the change of the seasons that follow one after another—a feeling of being close to, and dependent upon essential common knowledge in order to cope with or capitalize upon these changes—it may be easier to accept what I am about to say: Chaucer and his contemporaries saw time as a grand *circle*. Life was pictured as repetitive circles (rather like *years*) called "epicycles"; the center of the epicycles lay on the perimeter of a great circle. The progression of many epicycles followed one after the other, and ultimately the center of life *returned* once again to the point at which it had begun.

Lydgate, in his poem *Pilgrimage of the Life of Man*, reviews this sense of time.

> By the process of time long
> Thou shalt return again by grace
> Unto thine own due place,
> Rest in God, and there abide.

The progress of our personal epicycles, around this grand circle of "time long," is further clarified by Lydgate.

> And on the way, have in mind;
> Epicycles thou shalt find,
> Of misfortunes full of fevers,
> Of sudden predicaments very perverse;
> For thy life (there is no doubt,)
> Is like a circle that goes about,
> Round and swift as any thought
> Which in its course never ceases
> If he goes right, and circles well
> Till he comes to his resting place
> Which is in God, if he goes well
> [To] his own place which he came from.[305]

Life (a person's allotted time), after the epicycles have run their course, will come to rest finally at "his own place which he came from." Life begins, follows a circular path, and returns to the point at which it began. Time is a circle. These epicycles (years) also progress in a grand circle from Creation to Judgment.

(Earlier I noted parallels to a Corpus Christi Procession as the pilgrimage began with the closing lines of the *General Prologue*. This may be a thread of meaning that runs through the entire plan of the *Tales*. I mention this now because the procession, like our pilgrims, would be expected to return to the point of setting forth; the Eucharistic Host would be returned to the sanctuary of the church from which it had been removed.[306] In considering a possible Corpus Christi element we would need to make note of all possible connections—events, personages, places—to the plays that commemorated God's plan from Creation to Judgment, which were also performed on that feast day. A brief perusal of the Chaucer concordance finds mention of Adam and Eve in Paradise, Noah and the flood, Joseph, Mary, Herod, Caesar, Magdalen, Satan, the house of hell, and heaven and ever-present judgment. Of course a brief perusal is not what is needed, nevertheless it's a place to start. But enough of the circle of the procession.)

We return to the circular image of time. Chaucer was well acquainted with calculations involving the cycle of the year. He produced a work of instruction on such matters called *Treatise on the Astrolabe*; an astrolabe is an instrument inscribed with "a circle of days [which] follows the circle of the names of the months." This circle indicates, among other things, the sun's position for each day of the year. When the sun (on its circular path "around the earth") returns to a given point, a year has elapsed. Chaucer's Parson, in a spiritual sense, expresses the passage of time: "from one Easter day to another Easter day."[307]

Easter is the day of days in the Christian world. Not only does it transcend time and space as the culmination of Christ's salvific mission, but it keeps ecclesiasts busy because the calculation of its date each year is very complex; and the outcome of the calculation determines the date of many other feast days for that particular year. For our purposes, recall that the *Lay Folks Catechism* instructs that each man and woman "ought to receive [the Eucharist] once in the year / That is to say at paschal season (Easter)."[308] So the reception of the Sacrament of the Altar (the participation in the Lord's Supper)—our perfect food—is to occur once a year. Then this too is a cyclic pattern. We see this circular pattern in the *Canterbury Tales* when the "best vitaille" was provided by the Host at the beginning, and will be provided once again when their journey in time has come full circle, when they have returned to their point of origin.

It seems a comfortable way, for a man who had used an astrolabe, to envision returning to the same place. And the undue importance of an exact location specified by the Host seems to be a signal once again. The supper to be served upon their return will be "Here in this place, sitting by this post."[309] How strange to insist that they be at "this post." Why so specific? We can hardly imagine so large a group of people at one post—if we are thinking of *space*. But if we are to picture the group together at a precise point in *time*, our mind says, "Of course."

The detail of one certain post, a precise location or point of origin, brings the image of the astrolabe to mind. Chaucer, in his *Treatise*, repeatedly explains the importance of indicating a precise "point." Baldwin perceptively made us aware of Chaucer's "time-space continuum" in which the poet "boldly blurred the categories of time and space."[310] This is part of the covert plan. This time/ space point, that is noted so precisely, is Easter.

Why Easter? Because Chaucer's images point to the day. The

General Prologue began with allusions to March and April, the only two months in which Easter may fall. Then the pilgrims share "vitaille" of the best, which we have identified as the Eucharist. The following day the travelers waken early and the journey begins; the comparable ecclesiastic tradition noted is a form of pilgrim drama, a commemoration of Christ traveling with pilgrims, as a part of the Easter Monday services. Chaucer's specially gifted words—with both tangible and spiritual interpretations—are prepared for a dual performance here. The Host "rose up," which can intend *awaken;* but these little words hold the glory of the Resurrection, as well. They are shortly followed by the humble-looking "paas," which is a way of saying a *walking-pace;* but this modest word is illumined by an inner radiance, when it confides its alternate meaning—*Easter.* So, in *space* the pilgrims move at a little more than a modest *pace;* while in *time* they set out on Easter Monday, that is, "a little more than *Easter.*" Is there a more clever way to hide a reference to one day after Easter? The plan for their journey will bring them full circle in time, they will arrive again at Easter and be nourished once again by the Lord's Supper, which the Host has promised to provide.

I have stressed Chaucer's "designed vagueness," his ability to leave his characters free of physical attachments: food, lodgings, road conditions, problems with horses, etc. The poet refrains from inserting *things* into the surface story that would limit the travelers to an earthbound pilgrimage, thereby destroying the ambiguity. Lack of obstructions makes possible the symbolic view of a pilgrimage traversing the epicycle of the year to return to the point of origin in time. Here is the reason that the "thorp" (the last village before their destination) was left nameless. Naming a precise village would have bound them to earth/space.

Where does this leave the time/space travelers? For centuries the idea of pilgrimage "had the metaphorical significance of a one-way journey to the Heavenly Jerusalem: the actual trip was a symbol of human life, and the corollary, that life is a pilgrimage, was a commonplace."[311] Using the information that *time* was viewed as a circle, this one-way journey will take us right back to where we started, to our point of origin. The problem created by the apparent change in the Host's plan for stories to be told both going and coming no longer exists. He called for two stories outward bound and two homeward bound—but the outward journey *is* the homeward journey. Then the stories told moving away from that certain post were also told moving toward it. Now only two tales from each storyteller would be necessary.

The Host had asked that the stories contain "sentence and…solace"—a moral (a meaning reflecting doctrine) as well as entertainment or comfort. If we should find that the tales each have a double meaning (a surface entertainment, as well as the "sentence" called for) the Host will have heard the "two" stories at the same time (in best allegorical fashion) from each pilgrim going/coming.[312] (That still doesn't explain the pilgrims that are never heard from, but that will have to wait until another time/place.[313])

Each solution exposes a new problem, it seems. If this journey is symbolic, what happens to the Tabard? This is the final word in the game we've been playing, a "treasure" concealed within a loose-fitting, and humble exterior. We were in the Tabard at the beginning; we are to be there at the end. What sort of *reality* can we find in this? The "reality" is that the Tabard is a symbol, a deeply religious symbol.

One hardly notices, but Chaucer never refers to the "Tabard Inn." We alter the name without thinking, and feel comfortable doing so; the discovery of a "Tabard Inn" existing in fourteenth-century London makes it seem proper, makes us feel informed. And for Chaucer, the liberty taken with the name is all the better for concealing the covert intention. Chaucer's plan for the Tabard is simply to be a shelter for pilgrims, and it is where we expect to find the Host.

The word *tabard* is primarily associated with the Host, but Chaucer uses it (purposefully?) in one other place. One of the pilgrims, the Plowman, is said to wear a tabard, an indication of his poverty. This is an overgarment of coarse material, usually sleeveless, and worn by the lower classes and by monks. In Chaucer's day, it was the usual garb of poor men, and if we look to biblical and medieval evidence, Christ too is pictured as a poor man. Chaucer tells us that, "the high God in whom we believe, / In willful poverty chose to live his life." And Langland describes Christ's wearing "poor apparel and pilgrims clothing," which is also prescribed as Jesus' costume in the Chester play, where He joins the two disciples.[314] A tabard, then, would be accepted as a proper garment for Christ.

A simple image of Christ in a tabard is not difficult to fix in our mind's eye. The composite, however, of all the pilgrims sharing the Host's tabard seems beyond our "visual" capability. Such difficulty is to be expected. Comprehension is beyond us, because this is the portrayal of a *mystery*, "a doctrine of the faith involving difficulties which human reason is incapable of solving."[315] Chaucer's amazing inventiveness has captured a way of presenting the mystery of the Mystical Body—Christ and His members. Recall the lines quoted earlier: "Christ and His members / Are one body mystically." We considered the idea of Christ being the Head; the guests, His members. In the Host's Tabard, the pilgrims are part of the Body of Christ.

Though this may be a bit difficult to assimilate in the twentieth century, perhaps the following excerpts from *Festivals of the Church* will put it all in order. Alongside the first excerpt, the editor's explication in the margin reads: "The Lord is a householder; he feasts and clothes his folk."

I

The Lord who is a householder
With fair feasts folk he feeds
Giveth them clothes He Himself doth wear
On the bolster of the bed their troubles abate

. . .

With Him on the bed, man, thou sat
On the bolster of heavenly bliss.
With his flesh he feeds thee, thou knowest this well,
Thy soul shall be clad as His
In life that nevermore ends.

At the second portion, the editorial marginalia reads: "Thou hast worn thy Lord's garments."

II

. . .

He saith God is truly the Son
And in the same thy soul is clad
Thy Lord's garment then hast thou worn.[316]

For all of mankind to wear the garment of the Lord may seem a strange way of expressing relationship with God.[317] The oddity of it doesn't matter. What does matter is that medieval England thought in this way—and the reason for Chaucer's choice of the name of a *garment* for the pilgrims' shelter is captured in this remarkable festival poem. Chaucer's Host provides "feasts," "beds," and the "clothes he himself doth wear." Again we see the Host portrayed in actions which echo Christ.

These "echoes" are part of the allegorical technique. Selected descriptions and actions reverberate the hidden identity. Fletcher agrees with Elder Olson, who explains that "the allegorical incident happens, not because it is necessary or probable in the light of other events, but because a certain doctrinal subject must have a certain doctrinal predicate; its order in the action is determined not by the action as action, but by the action as doctrine."[318] To portray the Canterbury Host as the provider of food, drink, beds, is *necessary*. For the poet to have a felicitous inspiration of surrounding all the pilgrims with the Host's tabard (Tabard) may have surprised and delighted him as much as it did me, when the connection suddenly became clear. Echoing Christ can be seen as a strong determining element.

I am not alone in finding an image of God in Chaucer's work. The presence of Christ in the *Canterbury Tales* was felt more keenly by Baldwin than by any other author I've read. He feels Christ's image embedded in Chaucer's words, though the image has not completely revealed itself. He says, however,

Chaucer was conscious of the indivisible image, the Christ incognito under the features of these ill-assorted yet gloriously unific pilgrims....it is 'Christ who appears as a centre, an atmosphere, a whole world even' vivifying, unifying, communicating man and God, man and man. [319]

It is not the direct image of Christ that is perceived by Baldwin, but unmistakably the image of the Mystical Body. This excerpt from Baldwin was quoted earlier; it may hold greater meaning now.

One more poem is worthy of notice. It was an outstanding discovery for me, and may provide assurance of statements I have made. In preparation, I want to point out that although Chaucer does not use the image of a warrior-Christ within the Host (a commonplace of many medieval poems), we can have confidence that the poet was aware of the warrior image, because one of the pilgrims declares that, "Christ will be your champion and knight" against the "fiend."[320] With that last detail in place, compare Chaucer's Host with the following medieval thoughts from the poem, "How Christ shall Come."

> I come from the wedding as a sweet spouse,
>   who has brought my wife with me
> I come from the fight a stalwart knight,
>   who has overcome my foe
> I come from bargaining as a powerful chapman (businessman),
>   who has bought mankind
> I come from an unknown land as a blessed pilgrim,
>   who has searched over a great distance.[321]

The image of Chaucer's Host can be seen imprinted upon these lines. In fourteenth-century terms, the Host is the "lie" which covers the "truth" that is Christ. Chaucer's images were not unique; they were shared images. Christ was pictured coming as a spouse who has His wife with Him, as a stalwart knight in the harrowing of hell, as the businessman from Chepe, and in the parting vignette, as a simple pilgrim. This is how Christ came to Chaucer's mind, and to the *Canterbury Tales*.

It is the "fruit," the "sentence" that identifies our Host as Christ, mankind's sinless Guide, and Judge, and Shepherd, the Lord of Peace, the King of Bliss, and the Head of the Mystical Body.

A friend, familiar with my thinking, advised, "Limit your thrust to the idea of the Host as a type of Christ-figure, in order to

CHAUCER'S HOST: UP-SO-DOUN

gain wider acceptance." This would be a breach of integrity on my part. I know that Chaucer's countrymen encountered Christ Himself everywhere: in plays, songs, poems, homilies, carved figures, stained-glass windows, and—most important of all—as the Eucharistic Host, the Sacrament of the Altar. To say less than, "The Host is Christ," is to say nothing.

We must avoid the notion that all people must see the double meaning, for the work to be rightly called allegory. A least one branch of allegory...serves political and social purposes by the very fact that a reigning authority...does not see the secondary meaning.... But someone does see that meaning, and, once seen, it is felt strongly to be the final intention behind the primary meaning.

—Angus Fletcher, *Allegory: The Theory of a Symbolic Mode (1964)*

IX: A Conclusion

THE WORK OF art that is the *Canterbury Tales* has a new source of light coming from his carefully chosen words. Many of the figures we perceive, however, are still only silhouettes against a dim background. When the complete artistry of their rounded figures has become visible, we may understand more clearly why the Host's treatment of each pilgrim is so unique, so varied. That will have to wait until another time.

For now, this is the penultimate moment. Only one matter is left for examination. Did Chaucer have a particular reason for the complexities we've exposed? I am sure that at least in the structure surrounding the Host the answer is, "Yes." Yes, because something needed saying. The poet's "decoying realism" was "intended to shake off all but those hounds willing to follow Chaucer down the labyrinthine way of his art."[322] The way has surely been labyrinthine. The poet's words have led us down many pathways. Some, no doubt, had not been traversed for centuries.

We will prepare now for the drama promised in the beginning (p. 22). Comic figures will be asked to take positions off stage, as the curtain parts to spotlight the figure of the Host. We will see a man of stature, well-built, his eyes with a special quality. The voice we will hear is confident, at ease speaking to numbers of people, his words well-chosen and meaningful. All this Chaucer told us when our Host was introduced. But what shall we see as his garb? Details of clothing were withheld, so we will select as the Host's costume the one garment closely associated with him—the Tabard. This tall, confident figure in the dual role of Host/Christ—wearing a tabard, a simple, loose-fitting garment made of coarse material—will soon take his position at center stage. He will address his audience in two dramatic monologues, both on the subject of his wife. It is an important facet of Chaucer's plan, I am sure, that this wife is never *visible*. No multilevel scenes needed to be constructed. It was much easier just to incorporate ambiguities into a husband's observations.

The Host's first such observation follows Pilgrim Chaucer's story of Melibee's patient spouse, who is meaningfully named Prudence. On only one other occasion does the Host comment as a husband—when the Merchant has presented the story of deceitful young May, the wife of trusting old January. (With names like *May* and *January*, the discovery of an allegorical level seems inevitable.)

It will not be our purpose to see the Host's wife as a comic stereotype. Many decades of laughter have concentrated on her comic role and allowed a hidden meaning in the Host's commentary to be less detectable. Instead we will ask Bernhard ten Brink and Emile Legouis to set the mood by describing their impressions of the Host's wife. Professor ten Brink finds that the Host

> has a wife with a most violent temper, easily angered, and absolutely reckless in her rage. It looks as if she leads the Host a very bitter life.[323]

With similar, but even more penetrating words, Legouis strikes to the heart of Chaucer's plan, as he says of the Host's wife:

> What a dangerous tongue, and what a quarrelsome disposition! She must be an awe-inspiring creature with powerful arms, who fears no one, and before whom her lord and master, according to his own confession, is as *meek as a lamb*.[324]

I was not prepared for Legouis' surprisingly apt comparison of the

Host (Christ) to a *lamb!* Once again Chaucer's words bring forth the proper image, even though it fails to be recognized in its covert potential. Christ (as far back as the Wyclif Bible, 1389) refers to himself as *meek*. He is traditionally called the "Lamb of God."[325]

We must remember that as late as 1586, Chaucer was seen as a "bold spirit" dedicated to revealing problems by using "plain words," or else some "pleasant *covert*."[326] We've established the mood for our bold poet's words to be spoken. The scene is set. I will withdraw to the wings as the Host comes forward. Listen as he reacts, with dual intent, as a husband would to the story of patient Prudence, and as Christ expressing covert distress about his self-righteous wife—the Church:

> By God's bones! When I punish my servants,
> She brings forth to me the great club-like weapons,
> And cries, "Slay the dogs everyone,
> And break them, both back and every bone!"
>   And if a neighbor of mine
> Will not bow, be submissive, to my wife in church,
> Or be so fearless of danger as to offend her,
> When she comes home she attacks me to my face,
> And cries, "False coward, avenge thy wife!
> By corpus bones, I will have thy knife,
> And thou shalt have my distaff and go spin!"
> From day to night, just like that, she will begin
> "Alas!" she says, "that ever I was created, destined
> To wed a milksop, or a cowardly fool,
> Who will be deceived by every person!
> Thou dare not stand by thy wife's just claim, thy wife's law!"
>   This is my life, only if I will fight;
> Out the door at once, I must prepare myself,
> Or else I am lost, unless I
> Am like a wild lion, foolishly bold.
> I know well she will someday make me slay
> Some neighbor, and then go my way;
> For I am perilous with knife in hand,
> Although I dare not oppose her,
> For she is strong in her arms, by my faith:

That [is what] he shall find, who offends her by his deeds
    or words,
But let us pass away from this matter.[327]

And now reflections compare his wife to a deceiving wench:

But doubtless, as true as any steel,
I have a wife, though she be poor,
But of her tongue, she is a blabbering shrew, an evil-doer,
And yet she hath a heap of vices more;
Of that it doesn't matter! let all such things go.
But do you know what? In counsel (council) be it said,
I sorely rue that I am tied to her.
For, I should reckon, give account, of every vice
Which she has, in deed I am too wise;
And why? It would be reported
And told to her by someone of this group,—
Of whom, it need not be declared,
Since women perceive without such transactions;
And moreover my wits suffice not to it,
To tell it all, therefore my tale is done.[328]

When ten Brink and Legouis set the mood for us, they had unwittingly characterized the medieval Church: easily angered, absolutely reckless, awe-inspiring, powerful arms, fearing no one. The power of the Church, the tactics of the Inquisition, the self-protective fear directed against heretics, the misguided attempt to save souls by force,[329] the spiritual ordeal of Avignon vs. Rome—these were Chaucer's concerns of faith. His experience was not limited to England; he had traveled the Continent—eyes and ears open. How could he fail to ask himself, "Would Christ use these methods if He walked the earth today?" The poet says enough for us to understand, but breaks off—by changing the subject, or refusing to tell all—before the intention becomes transparent. It is the purpose, I'm sure, of many of his vagueries.

    One aspect of the medieval distress is described by H. C. Lea, an historian of the Inquisition. Torture had long been recognized as an effective tool. In the early 1300s Inquisitors asked to apply such methods without limitations to heretics, and thus "the Church grew harder and crueller and more unchristian." In a tone that seems to echo Chaucer's Host, Lea states, "to human apprehension the papal Inquisition was wellnigh ubiquitous, omniscient, and omnipotent."[330] This must have been Chaucer's "apprehension," as well. The Host's monologues seem to contrast the harsh, letter-of-the-law procedures of the fourteenth-century Church with Christ's Gospel message of love and justice.[331]

The message to his audience was mainly for the Church in England—the entire work is written in English and the destination of the pilgrims is England's mother church, not Rome. The Host's concern that someday he will be forced to slay a neighbor apparently refers to the poet's well-founded fear that the Inquisition would threaten England, Chaucer's *neighbors*. As mentioned earlier, just months after Chaucer's death an Englishman *was* burned at the stake.

The image of the Host/Christ as "perilous with knife in hand" brings the crucified Christ to my mind's eye: first, because *perilous* can mean *dreadful, fearful* as the sight of a tormented body hung on a cross; secondly, because the large nails of the Crucifixion have the appearance of knives *in* (not *held by*, but *piercing*) the hands of Christ. The medieval mind put a strange twist upon the implements of the Crucifixion. Associated with Christ as a knightly champion, these instruments of his death were recognized as the means of his victory. The cross, we know from an earlier chapter, was identified as his valiant steed. Consider next the lance that pierced Christ's side. Rather than a means of his destruction, it was seen as one of his weapons against Satan.[332] Then a hand pierced with a knife-like object would seem to fit this reversal pattern and be understood as a fearful threat, when the pierced hand belonged to Jesus.

Chaucer also gives passing but significant mention to the Church's power against those (himself included) who might offend by their *words* or *deeds*.

Turning our thoughts to the wife, when her behavior is compared to the trickery of May, she is found constant, as true as proverbial steel. But what a harsh simile—a wife like steel! A steel was an instrument to break marble, or strike fire from flint; steel was a way of referring to fetters (chains), all of these mental pictures reflect aspects of the medieval Church.

Then this wife is said to be *poor*, but we need not think, *impoverished*. Many types of characters can be poor. Gower explains, for example, that Avarice personified is poor because he never has enough. And Chaucer himself finds it a "great shame for a man to have a poor heart and a rich purse."[333] Poverty, we see, can express a spiritual rather than a pecuniary deficiency. And finally, the disclosure supposedly made in confidence (in counsel) that the Host/Christ is sorry to be married to this wife, can be read as a play on words spoken in *council*, intending church council.

The end of the fourteenth century must have been both an exhilarating and an excruciating time to be a Catholic—the developing splendor and pageantry; the oppressing terror and rigidity. Chaucer bequeathed this message about the Church to his readers. His salvation could depend on such courageous disclosures. Are other confidences concealed? Only time can provide the reply.

❦

When I began the pursuit of the image of Christ within Chaucer's Host, I had no idea where it would lead. The poem beckoned; I followed. Importance of the word *Host* in the fourteenth century is easily established. The word as "cousin" to the embodiment of Christ is also clear. Chaucer's reasons for constructing a second level of meaning are basic to his existence as a medieval writer—and helps to distinguish this as a great work of imagination, giving it a place above those of mediocrity.[334] The intricacy of the construction attests to his genius, and justifies his reputation with his contemporaries.

Jonathan Keates, writing about Canterbury Cathedral, remarks on the continuing inspiration of St. Thomas' shrine: "Writers have responded to the romance and heroism implicit in the story of one man's firm defiance of absolute authority…a man agonized by the need to choose between worldly advancement and spiritual recompense." Perhaps thoughts of Becket were the inspiration of Chaucer's literary pilgrimage.[335] Many would make the journey in thanksgiving for bodily cures attributed to the prayers of St. Thomas à Becket. Chaucer's intention might have been to ask Becket's prayers for courage and perseverance—to be able to present his message, no matter what the cost, and face death (if need be) as St. Thomas had.

Comedy of the *Canterbury Tales* has held the interest of audiences for generations. We may now be ready for the serious drama behind the curtain fashioned six hundred years ago by Geoffrey Chaucer.

NOTES

I: THE PROBLEM

1. *The Compact Edition of the Oxford English Dictionary*: Complete Text Reproduced Micrographically, 2 Vols. (Oxford: Oxford University Press, 1971). Hereafter cited as OED.

2. *The Tale of Beryn*, ed. F. J. Furnivall and W. G. Stone, Chaucer Society (London: N. Trübner and Co., 1887), Vol. 17. All quotations from the *Prologue of Beryn* are to this edition. The unknown, but enterprising, writer no doubt planned to capitalize on the established appeal of Chaucer's collection of pilgrimage stories by writing yet one more. It was to be told as the pilgrims began their return trip from Canterbury.

3. "Hoost of Southwork... / That was rewler / of hem al" (15–16); "Pese!... / Goith vp, & doith yeur / offerynge!" (157–58)

4. "Eche man as hym lest" (228); "wee erly rysen, our iourney for to do" (230); "al thing wrouȝt prudenciall, as a sobir man & wise; / 'Nowe woll wee to the souper...' / Quod the hoost ful curteysly" (381–83); "at a-countis, & [he] wexen som-what wroth. / But...preyd hem curteysly to reste for to wend." (420–21)

5. "Almyȝty sovereyn hath sent so feir / a day" (699); "grete gentilnes." (716) Entire celebratory section (681–99). "Litany" of reasons ll. 702–16.

6.
   As fer as I have saylid, riden, & I-go,
   Sawe I nevir man ȝit, to-fore þis ilch[e] day,
   So well coude rewle a company, as [can] our hoost, in fay.
   His wordis been so comfortabill, & comyth so in seson,
   That my wit is ovir-com, to make[n] eny reson
   Contrary to his counsaill, at myne ymaginacioune;
   Wher/for I woll tell a tale to yeur consolacioune;
   In ensaumpill to ȝewe; that when þat I have do,
   Anothir be all redy þen[ne] for to tell; riȝt so
   To fulfill our hoostis will, & his ordinaunce.

   (718–27)

7. Kemp Malone, *Chapters on Chaucer* (Baltimore: The Johns Hopkins Press, 1951), 191–92. Author's italics.

8. The problem results from point of view. Seeing the Host as

comically avaricious and devious unfortunately must color the impression of *all* his actions. An alleged fondness for money and profit in the Host's character is alluded to by many (we will see examples from Lumiansky, ten Brink, Legouis, and Keen), although there is no mention of *money* of any kind in the *General Prologue* or elsewhere, associated with the Host. And when the drawing of lots results in the Knight (the most distinguished pilgrim) telling his story first, some see this as *trickery* on the part of the Host, even though the narrator does not indicate underhandedness. See Bernard F. Huppé, *A Reading of the* Canterbury Tales (Albany, New York: State University of New York, 1964; rev. ed. 1967), 43: "we suspect...sleight of hand." See also J. S. P. Tatlock, *The Mind and Art of Chaucer* (New York: Gordian Press, 1966), 93: "there is a pretense of choosing the first tale-teller by drawing lots."

When one considers that the choice of the first storyteller is ultimately *Chaucer's*, and not an action of one of his characters, it seems much more reasonable to agree with Ralph Baldwin, that, "we have...in the selection of the Knight, evidence that Chaucer is, in spite of himself, a conservative...not modern at all, but explicitly mediaeval." ("The Unity of *The Canterbury Tales*," *Anglistica* 5, [1955]: 64.) The comic point of view will be covered in Chapter V.

II: THE PROPOSAL

9. G. K. Chesterton, *Chaucer* (London: Faber and Faber, 1934), 249; Miri Rubin, *Corpus Christi: The Eucharist in Late Medieval Culture* (Cambridge: Cambridge University Press,1991), 9.

10. Rubin, 348, 334.

11. Hardin Craig, *English Religious Drama of the Middle Ages* (Oxford: Clarendon Press, 1955), 130–33; E. K. Chambers, *The Mediaeval Stage*, 2 Vols. (London: Oxford University Press, 1903), II, 95. Italics added; Rubin, 10.

12. George Lyman Kittredge, *Chaucer and His Poetry* (1915; reprint, Cambridge, MA: Harvard University Press, 1946), 161, 164; Charles Muscatine, *Chaucer and the French Tradition* (Berkeley: University of California Press, 1957), 171; William Keen, "'To Doon Yow Ese': a Study of the Host in the *General Prologue* of the *Canterbury Tales*," *Topic* 17 (1969): 6; Rodney Delasanta, "The

Theme of Judgment in *The Canterbury Tales*," *MLQ* 31 (March 1970): 299. Hereafter cited as "Judgment."

13. Baldwin, 63.

14. There is a tradition which dates back to Scriptures, where Christ deals with people while remaining unrecognized. Mary Magdalene took the risen Christ to be a gardener (John 20:14–15). The disciples journeying to Emmaus thought Him just a pilgrim, a stranger (Luke 24:15–18). Christ is still portrayed literarily as a "stranger" among men.

15. *Allegory: The Theory of a Symbolic Mode* (Ithaca, NY: Cornell University Press, 1964; Cornell Paperbacks, 1970), 359.

III: Why Would Chaucer Create Covert Complexities?

16. Matthew 13:3–8; Mark 4:3–20; Luke 8:5–15; Fletcher, 311, 7.

17. W. T. H. Jackson, *The Literature of the Middle Ages* (New York: Columbia University Press, 1960), 320, 354; Huppé, 5–9; W. P. Ker, *English Literature: Medieval*, Home University Library of Modern Knowledge (New York: Henry Holt, [1912]), 184 ff.; George Saintsbury, *The Flourishing of Romance and the Rise of Allegory* (New York: Charles Scribner's Sons, 1897), 268.

18. Fletcher, 7.

19. "Many men ther ben that, with eres openly sprad, so moche swalowen the deliciousnesse of the jestes and of ryme, by queynt knitting coloures, that of the goodnesse or of the badnesse of the sentence take they litel hede or els none." D. W. Robertson, Jr., *A Preface to Chaucer: Studies in Medieval Perspectives* (Princeton, NJ : Princeton University Press, 1962; paperback, 1969), 287. Hereafter cited as *Preface*.

20. Huppé, 8.

21. *Five Hundred Years of Chaucer Criticism and Allusion 1357–1900*, ed. Caroline F. E. Spurgeon (Chaucer Society 1908–1917) 3 Vols. (Cambridge: Cambridge University Press, 1925; New York: Russell and Russell, 1960), I, 66–67. Italics added.

O, noble CHAUCER! euer most sure
Of fruitful sentence right delicious

. . .

he was expert
In eloquent terms subtle and couert.
(Stephen Hawes, [1503–4])

Spurgeon I: "In wytte and in good reason of sentence [Chaucer] passeth al other makers." (8)

22. Robertson, *Preface*, 287.

23. Derek Stanley Brewer, *Chaucer in His Time* (London: Thomas Nelson and Sons, 1963), 227; Sir Philip la Vache was advised not "to be thral" to the world, "Here is non home, here nis but wyldernesse." ("Truth: *Balade de Bon Conseyl*," 23, 17). *Chaucer's Major Poetry*, ed. Albert C. Baugh (New York: Appleton–Century–Crofts, 1963), 536–37. All citations to Chaucer's poetry from this edition, unless otherwise stated.

24. *Encyclopædia Britannica*, 1968 ed., s.v. "Jacquerie." Hereafter cited as *Britannica*.

25. Some quotes are from Walter Ullmann's introduction, and the remainder from the text of Henry Charles Lea, *The Inquisition of the Middle Ages: Its Organization and Operation* (New York: Harper Bros., 1901; New York: Harper and Row, Harper Torchbooks, 1963), 49, 31, 317, 35.

26. Fletcher, 326–28, 8.

27. Lea, 315–16.

28. *The Middle Ages: A Concise Encyclopædia*, ed. H. R. Loyn (London: Thomas and Hudson, 1989; paperback, 1991), s.v. "Plague"; *Britannica*, s.v. "Black Death."

29. Brewer, 60–61; John Masefield, *Chaucer* (Cambridge, England: Cambridge University Press, 1931), 23.

30. *Britannica*, s.v. "Lollards"; Roger S. Loomis, "Was Chaucer a Laodicean?" *Chaucer Criticism*: Vol. I *The Canterbury Tales*, ed. Richard Schoeck and Jerome Taylor (Notre Dame, IN: University of Notre Dame Press, 1960), 300.

31. Brewer, 233; Joseph Dahmus, *William Courtenay: Archbishop of Canterbury 1381–1396* (University Park: Pennsylvania State Uni-

versity Press, 1966), 100; Lea, 311–13; Loomis, 304.

32. Lea, 33–34; Rubin, 327–28.

33. "The sacrament was a central symbol or test of orthodoxy and dissent throughout the later Middle Ages." (Rubin, 9)

34. *Britannica*, s.v. "Bible, Translations of." Many regretted the availability of an English Bible. The chronicler, Knyghton, "deplored" the fact that the Bible, "the jewel of the church, is turned into the common sport of the people"; s.v. "Lollards"; s.v. "Wycliffe, John."

35. Delasanta, "Judgment," 300; John Lydgate, *Assembly of Gods*, ed. Oscar Lovell Triggs, EETS e.s. 69 (London: Oxford University Press, 1896), xlix: "this world is a thurghfare ful of woo"; "And thu shalt fynde this lyff *a pylgrymage*, / In which there is no stedfast abydyng." Author's italics.

36. Anne Middleton, "The Idea of Poetry in the Reign of Richard II," *Speculum* 53 (Jan. 1978): 102–03; Ernst Robert Curtius, *European Literature and the Latin Middle Ages*, trans. Willard R. Trask (New York: Pantheon Books, 1953; New York: Harper Paperback, 1963), 88. Curtius quotes Alan (*PL*, CCX, 586B):

    Non minus hic peccat qui censum condit in agro
    Quam qui doctrinam claudit in ore suam.

    (Not less sins he who hides his wealth in [a] field
    Than he who shutteth knowledge in his mouth.)

37. Loomis, 294.

38. Bloomfield quotes and clarifies Owst (*Preaching in Medieval England*): "there can be no single sermon by an Englishman of our two centuries [the fourteenth and fifteenth] of which so many copies in contemporary manuscript, and later printed book can be found." (87)
    The date of the sermon—1387 or 1388—is not certain.

39. Morton W. Bloomfield, Piers Plowman *as a Fourteenth-century Apocalypse* (New Brunswick, NJ: Rutgers University Press, [1962]), 87–89; Middleton, 102–03, n. 21.
    In comparing Langland's writing with that of the Lollard tracts, and Wimbledone's sermon, Bloomfield finds they all demonstrate that "the renewal of the world and Church, the same interest in Antichrist and the same belief in the imminence of a profound change in the Church, were by no means confined to

heretics."

40. "Ye shul alwey have thre thynges in youre herte ,/ that is to seyn, oure Lord God, conscience, and good name...yow moste have greet bisynesse and greet diligence that youre goode name be alwey kept and conserved" (VII 1615–45). Reiteration 1635–1650. All quotations to prose of Chaucer from *The Works of Geoffrey Chaucer*, ed. F. N. Robinson, 2d ed. (Boston: Houghton Mifflin, 1957).

    It was of utmost importance to maintain a good name where the Inquisition was concerned: "Direct proof was...not easily obtainable.... The witnesses appearing before the inquisitors were not therefore witnesses of fact, but witnesses of rumour, of the general reputation of the accused." (Lea, 44)

41. "I conseille that ye sende youre messages, swiche as been discrete and wise." (VII 1795–1805)

42. V. A. Kolve, *Chaucer and the Imagery of Narrative: the First Five Canterbury Tales* (Stanford, CA: Stanford University Press, 1984), 15–18. Hereafter cited as *Imagery*. Discussed in Huppé, 27.

43.
> So ofte a day I mot thy werk renewe,
> It to correcte and eke to rubbe and scrape;
> And al is thorugh thy negligence and rape.
>   (5–7)

    "Chaucers Wordes Unto Adam, His Owne Scriveyn"; Kolve, *Imagery*, 12. Author's italics.

44. Spurgeon, I: "Geffery Chaucer...was a sharpe Logician...a pure Poett, a graue Philosopher, and a sacred theologician...." (Unknown [1560], 95); "this is the very grounde of right poetrie, to give profitable counsaile, yet so as it must be mingled with delight." (Webbe [1586], 130); "I am partly informed of certain which knew the parties, which to them reported that by reading of Chaucer's works they were brought to the true knowledge of religion," and "[He] 'in mirth and covertly' was upholding the ends of true religion" (quotes Foxe [1570], xix–xx).

45. "An assumption of the right of censure by the Parliament which seems to have gone near to deprive us of Chaucer altogether." Francis Thynne, *Animadversions*, ed. G. H. Kingsley, rev. ed. F. J. Furnivall, EETS o.s. 9 (London: Oxford University Press, 1875; reprint, 1965), xiii–xiv; Thynne also writes, "When talke was had

of Bookes to be forbidden, Chaucer had there for euer byn condempned, had yt not byn that his woorkes had byn counted but fables." (10); Spurgeon, I: "I meruell to consider this, how that the Bishoppes condemnyng and abolishyng al maner of Englishe bookes and treatises, which might bryng the people to any light of knowledge, did yet authorise the woorkes of Chaucer to remayne...And therefore the Byshops, belike, takyng hys workes but for iestes and toyes, in condemnyng other bookes, yet permitted his bookes to be read" (Foxe, 105–06).

IV: How Could Chaucer Accomplish a Hidden Meaning?

46. Bloomfield, 3–6, 27, 147; Lydgate, *Assembly*, lxxv;

> Freewyll camc to Conscience,
>
> .   .   .
>
> "To Humylyte,"
> Quoth Conscience, "must þou go." So he hym thedyr sent
> Disguysyd that he were nat knowen as he went
> (*Assembly*, stanza 163)
>
> Answere yaue he noon to neyther party,
>
> .   .   .
>
> Hit hyng in hys balaunce the ambygyuyte.
> He seyde he wold nat restrayne hys lyberte.
>   When he come where sorow shuld awake,
>   Then hit shuld be know what part he woll take.
> (*Assembly*, stanza 145)

Another similarity can be seen between the ending of the first poem, *Piers Plowman*, and that of the *Canterbury Tales*. In *Piers*, "The poem deals with the search not the finding; ...the goal is yet to be attained" (Bloomfield, 3). An attainable goal (Canterbury) is yet to be achieved when the last of the Canterbury tales is completed.

47. John Livingston Lowes, *Geoffrey Chaucer* (Boston: Houghton Mifflin, 1934; Bloomington, IN: Indiana University Press, A Midland Book, 1958), 114; Brewer, 231; Ker, 228.

48. *Man of Law's Tale*:

155

Chaucer, thogh he kan but lewedly
On metres and on rymyng craftily,
Hath seyd hem in swich Englissh as he kan
Of olde tyme, as knoweth many a man.

(B47–50)

49. John Champlin Gardner, *The Construction of Christian Poetry in Old English* (Carbondale, IL: Southern Illinois University Press, 1975), 11.

50. Lowes, 156; Ker, 59–60; A. W. Ward and A. R. Waller, eds., *The Cambridge History of English Literature*, Vol. I (Cambridge: Cambridge University Press, 1908), 403. Oral tradition maintained some of the medieval stories on into the sixteenth century. See R. M. Wilson, *Early Middle English Literature*, 2nd ed. (London: Methuen, 1951), 295.

51. Ker, 247; "I kan nat geeste 'rum, ram, ruf,' by lettre." (I 43)

52. Gardner, 11–14. Gardner's examples of repetition are taken from Cynewulf and Chaucer.

53. Gardner, 13.

54. *Writers and Pilgrims: Medieval Pilgrimage Narratives and Their Posterity* (Los Angeles: University of California Press, 1980), 103; *General Prologue* A757, A759, A764, A766, A767, A773, A782, A802.

55. Robertson, *Preface*, passim. See index for additional Christian interpretations of Circe, Samson, Venus, the Sirens, Taurus, etc.

56. Ker, 186–87. Italics added.

57. Jackson, 354–55.

58. Edith Rickert's opinion is recalled in Robinson's note to line H50 in the *Manciple's Tale* (pp. 763–64).

59. "Ambages, / That is to seyn...double wordes slye, / Swiche as men clepen a word with two visages" (*Troilus and Criseyde*, V, 897–99); "Men may fynde... / ... / Whoso that hath the subtelte / The double sentence for to se." (*Romance of the Rose*, 7469–72); Kolve, *Imagery*, 41. Italics added.

60. Remarks of Walter Skeat in *The Academy*, No. 1139 (3/23/1894): 191.

A long castel with walles white,
Be seynt Johan! on a ryche hil

(1318–19)

61. *The Golden Legend of Jacobus de Voragine*, trans. Granger Ryan and Helmut Ripperger (New York: Longmans, Green, 1941; reprint, Salem, NH: Ayer, 1987); "Expowne" upon "Seinte Cecilie" (G87–119). Huppé, in turn, expounds on the process Chaucer uses: "The interpretations of the name proceed not as in modern etymologies from the word itself, the signifier, but from the signified. This etymological procedure is based on the theory that the word is 'cosyn' to what it signifies. Thus, to find the meaning of a word is to discover how it reflects the signified." (228) The same method needs to be applied to *host*.

62. Fletcher, 4.

63. W. J. Courthope, *A History of English Poetry*, 6 Vols., 4th ed. (London: Macmillan, 1895–1910; London: Macmillan, 1926), 366.

64. Opinion of Peter Levi, quoted on cover of *Geoffrey Chaucer: The Canterbury Tales,* ed. David Wright (Oxford: Oxford University Press, 1985).

65. Wolfgang Clemen, *Chaucer's Early Poetry* (New York: Barnes and Noble, Inc., 1964), 10.

66. John Ruskin, *Harbours of England* in *The Works of John Ruskin*, ed. E.T.Cook and Alexander Wedderburn, 39 Vols. (New York: Longmans, Green, 1904), 13, 21.

67. Bertrand H. Bronson, *In Search of Chaucer* (Toronto: University of Toronto Press, 1960), 18. See also Thomas Raynsford Lounsbury, *Studies in Chaucer: His Life and His Writings*, 3 Vols. (New York: Harper and Bro., 1892), III, 442; John Speirs, *Chaucer the Maker* (London: Faber and Faber, 1951), 104.

68. The Host's eagerness for financial profit is noted by: Baldwin 61–63; Keen, 13–14; R. M. Lumiansky, *Of Sondry Folk* (Austin: University of Texas Press, 1955), 221; Barbara Page, "Concerning the Host," *Chaucer Review* 4, No. 1 (1970): 11–12; Bernhard ten Brink, *History of English Literature*, trans. William Clarke Robinson, 2 Vols. (New York: Henry Holt, 1893), II, Part I, 147. David Wright gives an apparently needless translation of *made* (maad) as *paid* in an extension of this thinking (p. 20).

69. Fletcher, 72–73.

70. *General Prologue*, A783–87.

71. Kolve, *Imagery*, 5, 18; *General Prologue*, A822–24; Kolve, V. A., *The Play Called Corpus Christi* (Stanford, CA: Stanford University Press, 1966), 172–73. Hereafter cited as *Corpus Christi*.

72. Emile Legouis, *A History of English Literature 650–1660*, trans. Helen Douglas Irvine, rev. ed., 2 Vols. (New York: Macmillan, 1929), 1, 155; Grace E. Hadow, *Chaucer and His Times*, Home University Library of Modern Knowledge, No. 81 (New York: Henry Holt, [1914]), 84.

73. *The Writing Life* (New York: HarperPerennial, 1990), 75–76.

74. Altick, Richard D., *The Art of Literary Research* (New York: W. W. Norton, 1963), 103–04. Altick also stresses the fundamental necessity of mastering the vocabulary which was current when a work was produced.

75. E. T. Donaldson, ed., *Chaucer's Poetry: An Anthology for the Modern Reader* (New York: Ronald Press, 1958), 948; Huppé, 15.

76. Kolve, *Imagery*, 84.
   The tales that remain incomplete may have run into problems with the dual story line. It may be that when the double threads hit a snag, when no idea was forthcoming to continue working with both threads simultaneously, a tale was "abandoned," until a double-faced inspiration returned. If no method of dual continuity ever came to mind, the threads of the unfinished work were left dangling.

77. John Matthews Manly, *Some New Light on Chaucer* (New York: Henry Holt, 1926; Gloucester, MA: Peter Smith, 1959), 79–83.

V: WHY HASN'T THIS IDENTITY BEEN SEEN BEFORE?

78. Spurgeon I: "In goodnes of gentyl manlyche speche / without any maner of nycite of storieres ymagynacion in wytte and in good reason of sentence he passeth al other makers." (Thomas Usk [1387], p. 8) Chaucer's works as well as those of other fourteenth-century writers may just need to be taken "seriously." See also Middleton, 109.

79. Spurgeon I: "*Chawcer*, who for that excellent fame which hee obtayned in his Poetry, was alwayes accounted the God of English Poets (such a tytle for honours sake hath beene giuen him),...hath left many workes, both for delight and profitable knowledge, farre exceeding any other that as yet euer since hys time directed theyr studies that way." (William Webbe [1586], p. 129).

80. About stained glass, see Sydney A. Clark, *Cathedral France* (New York: Robert. M. McBride, 1931), 35–37. And especially Wim Swann, *The Gothic Cathedral* (Garden City, NY: Doubleday, 1969) regarding "ruby" glass "produced by a process whose secret has been lost" (62). About structure of cathedrals, regarding the secrets of construction among builders, and the idea that the existence of an architect is challenged, see Swann (83). Just for the joy of an exceptionally beautiful book, see all of Swann. Also see John Fitchen, *The Construction of Gothic Cathedrals: A Study of Medieval Vault Erection* (Oxford: Clarendon Press, 1961):

> The attempt will be made to discover something of the building procedures [medieval builders] evolved, something of the technical problems of erection they overcame in the actual operation of achieving the great thirteenth-century cathedrals, in so far as it is possible to do so at this time, some seven centuries after these fabulous structures were built. (1)

81. Speirs, 26; Robertson, *Preface*, 390.

82. Huppé, 7; *Munera Pulveris* in *The Works of John Ruskin*, ed. E.T. Cook and Alexander Wedderburn, 39 Vols. (New York: Longmans, Green, 1905), Vol. 17, 208; Robert P. Miller, "Allegory in the *Canterbury Tales*," *Companion to Chaucer Studies*, ed. Beryl Rowland Oxford: (Oxford University Press, 1968), 281; Jackson, 61; Robertson, *Preface*, 287–88.

83. Chesterton, in comparing Langland's work with Chaucer's Tales, demonstrates just how captivated a reader can be with the surface story: "The author of *Piers Plowman* denounces a variety of evils, indeed an almost universal conspectus of evils; because the very form of his book is an account of something very like a Day of Judgment; and not an account of a casual ride of holiday-makers to Canterbury." (247) The sentence of the Tales is completely overlooked.

84. Spurgeon I, xxix. Later, referring to "[Chaucer's] delightful humour,...his simplicity, his tenderness, his wisdom, toleration and broad-mindedness, his close knowledge of human nature, and his almost constant felicity of expression," Spurgeon points out that "with curiously few exceptions, from the middle of the sixteenth [century] to the end of the eighteenth century, not one of these qualities seems to be remarked in Chaucer. All his early admirers understood and praised his verse, but, as we have seen, in later years that found no support." (I, liii)

85. Spurgeon says of Dryden's essay on Chaucer that it tells us of Chaucer's greatness as a writer, as well as Dryden's greatness as a critic. (I, cxxxi–cxxxii); Spurgeon, I, xlv.
   In Spurgeon II, Part II, *Gentleman's Magazine* (1818), p. 94; William Wordsworth letter to Henry Reed (1841), p. 242; Part III, John O'Hagan lecture (1864), p. 73.

86. Adolphus William Ward, *Chaucer* (New York: Harper and Bros., [1887]), 153; Loomis quotes Coulton, 292; Spurgeon II, Part III, Furnivall, 1865; John Matthews Manly, *Canterbury Tales by Geoffrey Chaucer* (New York: Henry Holt, [1928]), 657; Lydgate, *Assembly*, xlii.

87. Emile Legouis, *Geoffrey Chaucer*, trans. L. Lailavoix (New York: E. P. Dutton, 1928), 200; Kittredge, 165; Ward, 167.

88. P. 249; Lounsbury, II, 466; ten Brink, 140; Spurgeon II, Part III: Even when a reviewer seemed to strive to be unprejudiced, his language exposed his leanings as he said he had come to no conclusion whether Chaucer had died "a Papist or a Protestant." (Rev. Gilfallen memoir [1860], in Tyrwhitt's edition of the *Canterbury Tales*, p. 52.)

89. Lounsbury, II, 466.

90. Rodney Delasanta, "Penance and Poetry in the *Canterbury Tales*," *PMLA*, 93, No. 2 (March, 1978): 240, nn. 1, 2. Hereafter cited as "Penance."

91. Jackson, 354; "Wikkid-Tunge seith never well," (3802), Robinson, 600; Robertson, *Preface*, 286, and 311 (n. 51), 390; Jackson, 355.

92. Robertson, *Preface*, 287–88.
   Angus Fletcher explains that "modern empirical science... depends in part upon the disjunction of creative (imaginative and

synthetic) and interpretive (empirical and analytic) mind, a major intellectual shift which might explain the modern distaste for allegory." (135)

93. When the "literal surface" becomes sufficient "the reader senses freedom from iconographic control." (Fletcher, 317) If we give up our "freedom," control reverts to the author, and we are challenged to seek the key, the nucleus, the treasure concealed.

94. D. Wright, 12.

95. Lumiansky, *Sondry*, 93; Manly, *Canterbury Tales*, 634; Kittredge, 31; Ker, 229.
   I was no specialist in the beginning; it was sheer fascination that urged me on.
   A stifling opinion of didactic medieval allegory was expressed (in 1896) by an editor of Lydgate's *The Assembly of Gods*: "We can now consider these works hardly other than monuments of the bad taste that accompanies a low literary culture." Those who once enjoyed these poems are found to have "the imperfect literary sense of the late Middle Ages in England...the Dark Age." (xli)

96. George Saintsbury, *A History of Criticism and Literary Taste in Europe*, 3 Vols. (New York: Dodd, Mead, 1900), I, 477; "A litel jape that fil in oure citee" (A4343); Robinson, 689; ten Brink, 155; Paull Baum, *Anglo-Saxon Riddles from the Exeter Book* (Durham, NC; Duke University Press, 1963), 57 ff., where the riddles can be understood as innocent or obscene, according to one's inclination.

97. Ten Brink sees "worthless speech...not worth a clod" (175) while Chaucer's words address *filthy speech...not worth a turd!* (B2113, B2120); Saintsbury insists "we do *not* know" why the Host interrupts the Tale (*History*, 451. Author's italics.), and yet Chaucer makes it clear. We need only accept the Host's protests.

98. Malone, 191–92; Keen, 16–17; Miller, 280.

99. Ten Brink, 147; Keen goes so far as to imply that the offer to guide them without recompense is a sham (13); Lumiansky, *Sondry*, 25; R. M. Lumiansky, "Chaucer's *Canterbury Tales, Prologue*, 784–787," *Explicator* 5, No. 3 (Dec. 1946): No. 20.
   There are other distorting speculations promoted for the sake of comedy, such as questioning whether the Host's wife has been

"faithful to him," (Malone, 191) or specifically if her "virtue ever suffer[ed] at the hands of [a monk]." (Legouis, *History,* 178–79) This is not mentioned or even hinted at by the narrator. This "reading into the lines" puts a different light on the Host, his wife, and the atmosphere of the *Tales.*

100. Charles A. Owen, Jr., *Pilgrimage and Storytelling in the* Canterbury Tales: *the Dialectic of "Ernest" and "Game"* (Norman, OK: University of Oklahoma Press, 1977), 20–23; Malone, 197.

VI: What Makes Discovery Possible?

101. Allan Temko talks of the "Cult of Carts" in *Notre Dame of Paris: the Biography of a Cathedral* (New York: Viking Press, 1952; Viking Compass, 1959), 101.

   Swann also observes that "there is no mention of the pious volunteers at Chartres taking part in the *actual construction.* The picture of chanting volunteers piling stone upon stone, and the cathedral rising as an unselfconscious paean of praise, an expression of 'folk art' as it were, is a fabrication of the Romantics." (73, author's italics.)

102. See Fitchen, n. 80 above.

103. Spurgeon II, Part III, 100.

104. See n. 86 above.

105. See n. 12 above.

106. See n. 60 above.

107. *Middle English Dictionary,* ed. Hans Kurath and Sherman M. Kuhn, in progress (Ann Arbor, MI: University of Michigan Press, 1956–). Hereafter cited as MED.

108. See n. 21 above.

109. Vol. I, cxxiv–cxxv.

110. John S. P. Tatlock and Arthur G. Kennedy, ed. (The Carnegie Institution of Washington, 1927; reprint, Gloucester, MA: Peter Smith, 1963).

111. W. F. Bryan and Germaine Dempster, ed. (New York: The Humanities Press, 1941; reprint, 1958). Hereafter cited as *S and A.*

112. See Fletcher, n. 15 above. See Rubin, n. 9 above. Rubin, 1.

113. Altick, 17.

114. Donald R. Howard says these tales have "*always* been understood, deal with marriage or domestic harmony." (Italics added.) *The Idea of the* Canterbury Tales (Berkeley: University of California Press, 1976), 247. "Always" dates from 1908.

115. *Literature and Pulpit in Medieval England: A Neglected Chapter in the History of English Letters and of the English People* (Cambridge, England: Cambridge University Press, 1933), 537–40, 229. Hereafter cited as *Literature. Preaching in Medieval England: An Introduction to Sermons of the Period 1350–1450* (Cambridge, England: Cambridge University Press, 1926). Hereafter cited as *Preaching*.

116. Owst, *Preaching*, 360–62; *Wimbledone's Sermon* Redde Rationem Villicationis Tue: *A Middle English Sermon of the Fourteenth Century*, ed. Ione Knight Kemp, Duquesne Studies Philological Series, No. 9 (Pittsburgh, PA: Duquesne University Press, 1967), 1.

117. "Ʒelde rekenynge of þy baylie" p. 69 (136). See Matthew 12:36; "þe grete Anticrist schulde come in þe fourtenþe hundred ʒeer fro þe birþc of Crist, þe whiche noumbre of ʒeeris is now fulfillid not fully twelue ʒeer and an half lackynge" p. 116 (895–98); "who douteþ þat þe world nis at þe ende?" p. 113 (836); "Þanne schal Crist axke rekeninge." p. 124 (1038)

118. "Ʒif þou wilt now be recheles of þyn owen welfare and take noon hede of þis rekenyng, ʒif þat deþ take þe sodeynly so þat þou passe hennis in dedly synnes…Þerfore þe desire of so gret ioie and þc drede of so gret peyne…sholde make þe to þenke euermore þat þou shalt ʒeue rekenyng of þy baylie." pp. 70–71 (151–160); "He is nyʒ." p. 117 (900)

Speculum Christiani gave fourteenth-century Englishmen a similar message:

> Euery man schal ʒelde vp a streyte a-cownte and reson be-for god of all thynges that he has doon or spoken; be whych helpes, bi what meryte, and by what entente he has comen to any state or degre; hou he has entrede, hou he has lyuede, hou he has perseuerede; what he has lernede, what he has taught, and in what doctrine he has continuede. (p. 54)

Speculum Christiani, ed. Gustaf Holmstedt, EETS o.s. 182 (London: Oxford University Press, 1933).

119. Bloomfield, 157; Heiko A. Oberman, "Fourteenth-Century Religious Thought: a Premature Profile," *Speculum* 53 (Jan. 1978): 82.

120. Kolve, *Corpus Christi*, 173–74.
    Chambers, *The Mediaeval Stage* is also an important source of secondary information about plays of the Middle Ages. Publications of the Early English Text Society (and others) provide the actual texts to examine and enjoy.

121. Derek Pearsall, *The Times Higher Education Supplement*, quoted on cover of Kolve's *Imagery*; Kolve, *Imagery*, 2–3, 63–64.

122. Kolve, *Imagery*, 63, 360–61.

123. Altick, 104; Lowes, 54–55.

124. Malone, 12.

125. Brewer, 230–31; H. S. Bennett, *Chaucer and the Fifteenth Century* (Oxford: Clarendon Press, 1947), 100; Oberman, 90–93; Delasanta, "Judgment," 301.

126. Howard, *Idea*, 52. Howard continues (referring to *Key of Remembrance*), "Professor Payne has demolished this estimate of the tales by tabulating the amount of seriousness in their content—there is more than four times as much (by sheer bulk) as there is of humorous content."; Loomis, 306.

127. Chesterton, 249; Walter L. Wakefield and Austin P. Evans, ed. and trans., *Heresies of the High Middle Ages* (New York: Columbia University Press, 1969), 376–77. Inquisitors connected to the Inquisition in France were imported temporarily to England to deal only with the case of the Knights Templar in the early 1300s.
    See n. 88 above for the direct, but anachronistic, question of Chaucer's Catholic vs. *Protestant* allegiance.

128. Kolve (quoting J. A. W. Bennett), *Imagery*, 389–90, n. 60.
    The difference of opinion, Kolve expresses, involves "a long section remarkable not for any particular poetic eloquence or power...but for the ambiguity with which it registers the mode of experience being described." (p. 41) The fact that such an ambiguous passage is recognized still does not explain why such a style was used.

129. Baldwin, 32, 90; "as I lay / Redy to wenden on *my* pilgrymage" (A20–21, italics added). This might find Chaucer's two stories (Pilgrim Chaucer, that is) the focal point of the collection, but

that is beyond our present topic.

130. "Preye for me that Crist have mercy on me and foryeve me my giltes"; "that sownen into synne"; "oure Lord Jhesu Crist"; "that I may been oon of hem at the day of doom that shulle be saved." (Robinson, 265); Baldwin, 99.

131. Kolve, *Imagery*, 371.

132. The Host's words are, "But hasteth yow, the sonne wole adoun." (I 70)

Though Middleton speaks mainly of Gower and Langland, her impression of late fourteenth-century poetry as a "realization of the human condition" relates to Chaucer as well. (108–10) If we accept the serious side of Chaucer's words, another view of his world is accessible to us.

Kolve, in his summary regarding imagery in the *Canterbury Tales* says, "If…art is part of man's quest for grace—grace understood as a kind of integration, a sense of speaking and feeling from an integrated center—then it is easy to see how that quest, in an age of faith and a theocentric culture, would often merge into, or return to, the religious quest itself." (371)

133. Speirs, 99; Baldwin, 104, 39.

134. Baldwin, 27–28, 74.

135. Kolve, *Imagery*, 83.

136. Huppé, 240; Speirs, 137; Delasanta, "Judgment," 302; "Of aventures that whilom han bifalle" (A795); Howard, *Idea*, 157.

137. Kolve, *Imagery*, 4.

138. Howard, *Writers*, 97. Howard reiterates that "until Furnivall (1868) critics spoke as if the journey took place all on one day." (125)

139. Malone, 194–95; Howard, *Writers*, 79; Delasanta, "Penance," 246.

140. Baldwin, 30, 32, 57.

141. Baldwin, 84. Author's italics.

142. Angus Fletcher, in discussing the value and intention of allegory, asserts that in times of repressive control (such as an Inquisition or a Merciless Parliament) "some sort of allegorical subterfuge is possible." In the late 1300s, then, a writer could speak through

allegory to meet the challenge of censorship.

The study explains that an allegorical story "often has a ...*peculiar doubleness of intention*." (7, italics added) This "peculiar doubleness" has been my experience with the *Canterbury Tales* from the moment we were introduced.

Fletcher cites examples of allegory existing in ancient classical literatures, as well as Prudentius' *Psychomachia*, Dante's *Divine Comedy*, John Bunyan's *Pilgrim's Progress*, Edmund Spenser's *Fairie Queene*, and on into present-day literature, poetry, films, etc.

143. Huppé, 239; Speirs, 25; Miller, 279, 288; Kolve, *Imagery*, 71; Huppé, 9.

VII: WHAT ARE THE CHARACTERISTICS OF THE 14TH-CENTURY IMAGE OF CHRIST?

144. Kolve, *Corpus Christi*, 173.

What Kolve says of medieval dramatists seems very appropriate for Chaucer as well. He speaks of the imagination bound up in the actions and characters:

So thoroughly is the theological background assimilated that *we seem to be in the presence of nothing more than ordinary life, closely observed and represented*. But the realism of these comic actions is, as a medieval metaphysician might say, accident, not substance." (*Corpus Christi*, 174. Italics added.)

Accident and substance will play an important part in Chapter VIII to follow.

145. Kolve, *Corpus Christi*, (quotes Augustine) 109, 106; Courthope 403; *The Middle English Harrowing of Hell and the Gospel of Nicodemus*, ed. William Henry Hulme, EETS o.s. 100 (London: Kegan Paul, Trench, Trübner and Co., 1907), 817; 1657–68. Hereafter cited as *Harrowing* or *Nicodemus*, respectively.

In "Cristes Passioun," we find that Christ "Stood afore bisshopes" and "Herowdis" and "Pilatys." *The Minor Poems of John Lydgate I*, ed. Henry Noble MacCracken, EETS e.s. 107 (London: Keegan Paul, Trench, Trübner and Co., 1911), 219, ll. 56-69.

146. Kolve, *Corpus Christi*, 50; *Britannica*, s.v. "Corpus Christi"; Chambers, II, 95. The importance of the feast has continued through the centuries. Mozart wrote his "Ave Verum Corpus" for

the occasion of this feast.

147. The fourteenth century recognized Aquinas as source of the most popular Roman office for the feast. The style of the readings, Old Testament as prefiguring the Eucharist, Thomas' confessor's testimony, representations of Thomas holding the liturgy in contemporary works of art, all demonstrate that his authorship was recognized. (Rubin, 185–195)

148. Fletcher, 5; Rubin, 1; 25, 53–55 (italics added), 92–93, 226.

149. Kolve, *Corpus Christi*, 48.

150. Glynne Wickham, *Early English Stages: 1300 to 1660*, 2 vols. in 3 (New York: Columbia University Press, 1959), I, 313; Chambers, II, 95.

151. Wickham, I, 58. Such a "stage" was the water conduit in Cheapside. Several other conduits (and the like) were built after 1377. See illustration Wickham, I, 57.

152. Kolve, *Corpus Christi*, 49; 287, n. 48.

153. Modern English from the Martial Rose edition of *The Wakefield Mystery Plays* (New York: Doubleday, 1962; paper. New York: W. W. Norton and Co., 1969), 175–76. Middle English from *Towneley Plays,* ed. George England and Alfred W. Pollard, EETS e.s. 71 (London: London: Kegan Paul, Trench, Trübner and Co., 1897). Both quotations are from the beginning of "The Annunciation." "Begyled... / Thrugh the edder." (24–25)

> Bot yit, I myn, I hight hym grace
> Oyll of mercy I can hym heyt,
> And tyme also his bayll to beytt.
> ffor he has boght his syn full sore,
> Thise fyfe thowsand yeris and more,
> ffyrst in erthe and sythen in hell;
> Bot long therin shall he not dwell.
> Outt of payn he shall be boght,
> I wyll not tyne that I haue wroght.
> I wyll make redempcyon,
> As I hyght for my person,
> All wyth reson and with right,
> Both thrugh mercy and thrugh myght.

> . . .
>
> Ryghtwysnes wyll we make;
> I wyll that my son manhede take,
>
> . . .
>
> And I wyll that all prophecye
> Be fulfyllyd here by me.

(8–44)

154. John Mirk, *Mirk's Festial: A Collection of Homilies*, ed. Theodor Erbe, EETS e.s. 96 (London: Kegan Paul, Trench, Trübner and Co., 1905), 154.

155. *Ludus Coventriæ*, ed. K. S. Block, EETS e.s. 120 (London Oxford University Press, 1922).

> Now all mankende in herte be glad
> with all merthis þat may be had
> ffor mannys sowle þat was be-stad
>   in þe logge of helle;
> now xal I ryse to lyve agayn
> from peyn to pleys of paradyse pleyn
> þerfore man in hert be fayn
>   in merthe now xalt þou dwelle.

p. 305 (971–78)

156. *The Hours of the Divine Office in English and Latin*, 4 Vols. (Collegeville, MN: St. John's Abbey Press, 1963), II. Hereafter cited as *Divine Office*. The prayer is *Verbum supernum prodiens*:

> *Se nascens dedit socium,*
> *Convescens in edulium,*
> *Se moriens in pretium,*
> *Se regnans dat in præmium.*

(p. 1478)

Italics added to the English.

157. Kolve, *Corpus Christi*, 172–73.

158. F. C. Gardiner, *The Pilgrimage of Desire* (Leiden, Netherlands: E. J. Brill, 1971), 32, 86–87, 22, 13.

159. Gardiner, 86, 133, 155.

160. Gardiner, 48. The sermon now is recognized as Pseudo-Bernard.

161. *Miracles de Nostre Dame*, see Charles Mills Gayley, *Plays of Our*

Forefathers (New York: Duffield, 1907), 75; Rossell Hope Robbins, "Private Prayers in Middle English Verse," *Studies in Philology* 36 (July 1939): 473–74. Author's italics. Hereafter cited as *St. in Phil.*

162. Rossell Hope Robbins, "Popular Prayers in Middle English Verse," *Modern Philology* 36 (May 1939): 337. Hereafter cited as *Mod. Phil.*

> Iesu, for Thy Holy Name,
> And for Thy bytter Passioun,
> Saue me frome synne and schame
> And endeles dampnacion.

163. Robbins, *Mod. Phil.*, 341. These "two lines in particular [a prayer 'tag']…are found many times in other prayers":

> Lord, for Thynne Holy Name,
> Schelde me from worldes schame.

With slight variations, the two lines "must have had a tremendous circulation." (342)

164. The lasting impression is "the remarkable sanity of popular religion in the Middle Ages as revealed by the corpus of private vernacular prayers and by this group of popular prayers of the people." (Robbins, *Mod. Phil.*, 350)
    Rubin, 315, 162, 219.
    Chaucer, too, remarks upon the Holy Name: "'Ther nys noon oother name,' seith Seint Peter, 'under hevene yeven to men, in which they mowe be saved'; that is to seyn, but the name of Jhesu Crist." (I 595–600) And belief in the power of the name is also dramatized in the *Man of Law's Tale*. (B561 ff.)

165. Wickham, I, 313. The intention of the friars was to bring a new comfort and understanding to men, as well as to counteract heresies of the day.

166. Courthope, 403; Kolve, *Corpus Christi*, 32.

167. *Festivals of the Church*, an appendix in *Legends of the Holy Rood*, ed. Richard Morris, EETS o.s. 46 (London: N. Trübner and Co., 1871). Hereafter cited as *Festivals*.

> Hys flessche is oure faire feest,
>
> · · ·

> Almyȝty god omnipotent,
> Hys blessyd body haþ sent
> To fede hys freendys here.
>
> (31, 43–45)

168. Lydgate, *Minor Poems I*, p. 36.

> Fruyt celestyal hong on þe tre of lyff,
> þe fruyt of fruytes for shorte conclusyoun,
> Oure helpe, oure foode, and oure restoratyf
> And cheef repaste of oure redempcioun.
>
> (13–16)

169. "Hele of the worlde"; "brede of lyfe," from "A prayer to the sacramente," *Octaua tabula* in *Speculum Christiani*, 160.

170. Carleton Brown, *Religious Lyrics of the Fourteenth Century* (Oxford: Clarendon Press, 1924), No. 48:

> With noble mete he norysched my kynde,
> For with his flessch he dyd me fede;
> A better fode may na man fynde,
> For to lastand lyf it will vs lede.
>
> (29–32)

171. John Lydgate, *The Pilgrimage of the Life of Man*, ed. Frederick J. Furnivall, EETS e.s. 77, 83, 92 (London: Kegan Paul, Trench, Trübner and Co., 1899, 1901, 1904), 126. Hereafter cited as *Pilgrimage*:

> Wych Body I leve also
> To trewe pylgrymës that her go,
> As thyng that most may hem avaylle
> Hem to releue in ther travaylle;
> As cheff Repast, hem to sustene
>
> (4794–4801)

172. Brewer, 222.

173. *O pretiosum et admirandum convivium, salutiferum et omni suavitate repletum! Quid enim hoc convivio pretiosius esse potest? ...sed nobis Christus sumendus proponitur verus Deus.* (*Divine Office*, II, p. 1470).

174. *Pinguis est Panis Christi.* (*Divine Office*, II, p. 1478).

175. *Festivals*:

And with hys fleisshe þi goost is fed;
He let atame hys pyement tunne
To make his gode gestis glad,
With a spere of grounden gad;
Þan was founde a fell fawset,
In þe trie tunne it was sette,
In cristes hert was piȝt and pette,
Hys brest was al be-blad.*

pp. 210–11 (21–28)

*Although *blood-stained* is the usual translation of "be-blad," in this case, to render the words as *drained of blood* seems much more appropriate.

176. "Brede of lyfe"; "holy hooste"; "sacred verrey flesche"; "verrey man"; "oure ioye"; "myrth of herte." *Speculum Christiani*, 160; Kolve, *Corpus Christi*, 47–48.

177. *Lay Folks Catechism*, ed. Thomas F. Simmons, EETS o.s. 118 (London: Henry E. Nolloth, 1901), 66. Hereafter cited as *Catechism*.

the sacrement of the auter,
Cristes owen bodi in likeness of brede,
. . .
Whilk ilk man and woman, that of eld is,
Aught forto resceyve anes in the yhere,
That is at sai, at paskes, als hali kirke uses,
When thai er clensed of syn thurgh penaunce.

p. 66 (316–22)

Festivals, XXVIII, p. 220, 303. "Estren is oure ful fode."; *General Prologue*, A749.

178. *Ludus Coventriæ*, The Appearance to Luke and Cleophas:

Jhesus. Well ovyr-take ȝe serys in same
to walke in felachep with ȝow I pray.
Lucas. welcom serys in goddys name
of good felachep we sey not nay.

p. 338 (41–44)

Christus. Beth mery and glad with hert fful fre
ffor of cryste jhesu þat was ȝour ffrende
ȝe xal haue tydyngys of game and gle

p. 343 (209–11)

179. Rose, 483; "Where euer is gam and play; / Of that myrth shall he neuer mys." Towneley, XXVII, 231–32.

> All that the prophetys told to you
> before, it is no trane.
> Told not thay what wyse and how
> That cryst shuld suffre payn?
>
> .   .   .
>
> Thay saide ihesus to ded shuld go,
> And pynde be on roode;
>
> .   .   .
>
> his woundys rynyng on red blode;
>
> .   .   .
>
> Crist behovid to suffre this,
> fforsothe, right as I say,
> And sithen enter into his blys
> vnto his fader for ay.
>
> p. 332 (212–29)

180. "Dialogue between Jesus and the B. V. at the Cross." Brown, No. 67.

> Maiden & moder, cum & se,
> þi child is nailed to a tre;
> hand & fot he may nouth go,
> his bodi is wonden al in wo.
>
> (1–4)

181. Oberman, 85; *The Chester Plays*, II, ed. Dr. Matthews, EETS e.s. 115 (London: Kegan Paul, Trench, Trübner and Co., 1916), XIX, "God may of his maiesty / doe what soeuer hym lyst." p. 353 (31–32); XXIV, "Lord, I must dreed thee / ... / for thou art most in maiesty." p. 430 (73–75); "Pearles Prince of most Posty." p. 432 (141); "Lord of lordes, and kinge of kinges / ... / thy power, lord, spreads and Springes." p. 431 (109–11)

182. "The godhede went untill hell, / And heried it," *Catechism*, p. 28; "Sunne (sin) ne foundest þou neuer non / *In me* as in anoþer mon." Italics added. *Harrowing*, p. 8 (63–64)

183. *Cursor Mundi*, ed Richard Morris, EETS, o.s. 57, 59, 62, 66, 68 (London: Kegan Paul, Trench, Trübner and Co., 1874–1878; reprint, London: Oxford University Press, 1966).

> clerli spac he quat he walde.

> & his skille wiseli he talde.
> In his snaiping aghful was he.
>
> (18851–53)

184. Rose, p. 483; Towneley, XXVII

> Ihesus: ye foyles, ye ar not stabyll!
>   where is youre witt, I say?
> wilsom of hart ye ar vnabyll
>   And outt of the right way,
> ffor to trow it is no fabyll
>   that at is fallen this same day.
>
> pp. 331–32 (202–07)

185. Stage directions in Chester II, XIV, following 224 and 260 both indicate scourging; "you make my fathers wonninge / a place of marchandiye" p. 258 (227–28); "I Iye you fast this Temple fro!" p. 259 (261); *Chester Plays*, Vol. I, ed. Hermann Deimling, EETS e.s. 62 (London: Oxford University Press, 1892; reprint, 1926), XIII, 265; Chester II, XIX, 73; *Harrowing*, "Wer is nou þe ȝateward? / Ich holde him for a couard." p. 12 (129–30); "Ich haue Iherd wordes harde, / ... / Ich lete hem stonden and renne away." p. 12 (131–36)

186. "If thow be knowynge evyn with all-miȝty God in witt, powere and wisdome, then thu myȝt swere as God ded." Owst, *Literature*, 420.

187. "*The Second Shepherd's Play:* A Reconsideration," *PMLA* 93 (Jan. 1978): 84. Author's italics.

188. Brown, No. 51: "Mi palefrey is of tre, / wiht nayles naylede ȝwrh me. (13–14); Rose, pp. 396, 399; Towneley, XXIII, "we shall sett the in thy sadyll" (102); "Stand nere, felows, and let se / how we can hors oure kyng so fre," (107–08); "I hope he & his palfray / Shall not twyn this nyght." (201–02)

189. Chester, II, XXIV: "*Stabunt Angeli cum Cruce, Corona Spinea, lancea, aliisque Instrumentis, omnia demonstrantes.*" (follows 356), and "*Tunc emittet Sanguinem de Latere suo.*" (428); Towneley, XXIII, "I thus for the haue blede." (474)

190. Brown, No. 76:

> al...for þi sake.
>
> . . .

þe nailes, þe scourges, & þe spere,
þe galle, & þe þornes sarpe—
Alle þese moun witnesse bere
Þat i þe haue wonnen with myn harte.

(4–24)

Brown, No. 51:

Biheld mi side,
mi wndes sprede so wide,
Rest-les i ride.
lok up on me! put fro ȝe pride.

(9–12)

Brown, No. 47:

Man, I luf þe ouer all thing,
And for þi luf þus wald I hyng,
My blyssed blode to blede.

(4–6)

Brown, No. 77:

Pyned, nayled, & done on tre—
All, man, for þe lufe of þe.

(23–24)

Brown, No. 55:

þe crune of ioyȝe vnder þornes lay.

(26)

Brown, No. 40:

swete be þe nalys,
and swete be þe tre,
and sweter be þe birdyn þat hangis vppon the!

(5–8)

Brown, No. 67:

On rode (rood, cross) i hange for mannis sake,
Þis gamen alone me must pleyȝe

(18–19)

191.

A voyce spak þan full hydusly,
Als it war thonours blast:
"vndo yhour yhates bilyue, byd I,
þai may no langer last,

þe kyng of blys comes in yhow by."

(1381–85)

þan Ihesus strake so fast,
þe yhates in sonder yhede
And Iren bandes all brast.

(1402–04)

Ilk prophete þus gan tell
Of þair awen prophecy
How he suld hery hell,
How he suld for þam dy.

(1533–36)

192. *An Anthology of Old English Poetry*, trans. Charles W. Kennedy (New York: Oxford University Press, 1960), 145.

193. Brown, No. 25:

What ys he, þys lordling þat cometh vrom þe vyht
Wyth blod-rede wede so grysliche ydyht,
So vayre y-coyntised, so semlich in syht,
So styflyche ȝongeþ, so douhti a knyht?

Ich hyt am, Ich hyt am, þat ne speke bote ryht,
Chaunpyoun to helen monkunde in vyht.

(1–6)

194. Rose, 344.

195. Rose, 385; Towneley, XXII:

Mans saull that I luffyd ay / I shall redeme securly,
Into blis of heuen for ay / I shall it bryng to me.

p. 254 (328–29)

196. *York Cycle of Mystery Plays,* ed. J.S. Purvis (London: SPCK, [1957]), 328.

197. Gardiner, 49.

198. *The Exeter Book: An Anthology of Anglo-Saxon Poetry*, ed. Israel Gollancz, EETS o.s. 104 (London: Kegan Paul, Trench, Trübner and Co., 1895), p. 55 (868–73).

199. Italics added to Modern English.

Leon men mai him clepe wid right,
For mai na best be mare of might.
And alsua þar es oþer resun
Qui he es takened to a leon,

．　．　．

Of leon alsua þe kind es hey,
Slepand loukes he neuer his eie,
Ne iesus, þou his gast he ȝald
His godd-hede þat has all i[n] wald,
Moght neuer dei ne neuer sall,
Ne slepe, þat has to wake vs all.

(18641–60)

See also *The Middle English* Physiologus, ed. Hanneke Wirtjes, EETS o.s. 299 (Oxford: Oxford University Press, 1991), 3. Hereafter cited as *Physiologus*.

200. For example: Chester II, XXIV, 412; *The Stanzaic Life of Christ*, ed. Frances A. Foster, EETS o.s. 166 (London: Oxford University Press, 1926), 4491. Some instances are: Brown, Nos. 21, 22, 23; Robbins, *Mod. Phil.* and *St. in Phil.*, passim; *Stanzaic Life*, 4000, 4184, 4477. See also OED, s.v. "forbuy"; MED, s.v. "forbiing."

201. MED, s.v. "rekenen" 3. e. Matthew 18:23. *Wyclif Bible 2* (1395): "The kyngdom of heuenes is licned to a kyng that wolde rekyn…with hise seruauntis." *Rekenen* has many connotations involving verbal statements, monetary dealings, and more. Examples are: relate (something), recount; narrate (a story); describe, tell, speak, declare; calculate a sum, count up money; give an accounting, hold an audit; answer for one's conduct; settle accounts; fig., make atonement.

Wimbledone sermon: "þou shalt ȝeue rekenyng of þy baylie," p. 71 (159–60); "ȝelde rekenyng of þy balie." p. 75 (232)

The St. Paul sermon also uses the alternate phrase, directing: "ȝeue now þyn acounte." (p. 76) This is followed by questions relating to the treatment of those under one's care, the use of profanity, concern for fatherless children, etc. The *accounting* is not devoid of considerations of the money one has been given, but it is much more all-encompassing.

202. *Cursor Mundi*:

vche of vs witturly

Haþ receyued goddes tresory

Riche besauntis (talents)of golde þei ben

Somme lasse & somme moo to sen

Þo besauntis so þat we biset

Þat we may wel paye oure det

To acounte....

            .   .   .

He ȝyue vs grace so to acounte

Þat we may to heuen mounte.

(23883–94)

203. XXIV "reconinge of the right" p. 427 (10); "reckon their deedes"
p. 445 (515); Wickham, I, 318.

204. Owst, *Literature*, 519.

205. *Confessio Amantis of John Gower*, ed. Reinhold Pauli, 3 Vols. (London: Bell and Daldy, 1857), 2. The "ende of oure accompte, /
Which Crist him self is auditour." (p. 191)

206. *Ludus Coventriæ*, "now xal we dwellyn in blysful place / In joye
and endeles myrthe." p. 318 (1354–55); *Speculum Christiani*,
"myrth of herte." (p. 160); *Exeter*, Day of Judgment, 1198;
Towneley XXV, "My fader me from blys has send / Till erth for
mankynde sake" (1–2); Chester II, XXIV, "I bledd to bringe you
to blis" p. 442 (431); *Cursor Mundi*, "kyng of blis" (18131); Mirk,
"gladyþ all," "makyþe myrþ" (131); Towneley XXV: "A kyng of
blys that hight ihesus." (198)

207. *Catechism:*

if we wele do whiles we er here,

Wend with god to that blis that euermare lastes,

And als if we iuel do, til endeles payne.

p. 26 (115–17)

208. The Day of Judgment in the *Exeter Book* sounds much more biblical and threatening about being awakened:

With sudden fear, at midnight then,

the mighty Lord's great day,

shall boldly strike earth's inhabitants

and the bright creation, even as some wily robber,

some daring thief that prowleth in the dark,

in the swart night, surpriseth suddenly
careless mortals bound in sleep
(867–73. Italics added)

> Þe day of doom hit callen men
> wheþer þer be mo þen oon þen
> Vndir þe name of day men shalle
> vndirstonde þe tyme þat alle
> Shal be demed at doom so strong
> wheþer hit laste short while or long.
> (23013–18)

209. *Stanzaic Life*, 131–33; *Golden Legend*, 134.

210. "Oure lorde putt thre questiouns to his spouse, and seid, "I am thy makere, and thy lorde; telle me thre thinges that I aske of the." (424). *The Early English Version of Gesta Romanorum*, ed. Sidney J. H. Herrtage, EETS e.s. 33 (London: Trübner and Co., 1879), XCIV.

VIII: DOES CHAUCER'S HOST FIT THIS IMAGE OF CHRIST?

211. Baldwin, 104.

212. Malone, 159.

213. MED, s.v. "brod(e"; "Crist spak hymself ful brode in hooly writ, / And wel ye woot no vileynye is it." (A739–40)

214. Muscatine, 171.

215. Lumiansky, *Sondry*, 87; Malone, 172. The Host's words are:

> ...if yow liketh alle by oon assent
> For to stonden at my juggement
> (A777–78)

> And whoso wole my juggement withseye
> Shal paye...
> (A805–06)

216. There was apparently "little interest in criticism in the Middle Ages." Theologians took literature to be a handmaid to theology and philosophy; rhetoricians examined "technical matters." Although Italy can boast Dante, Boccaccio, and Petrarch, who "produced critical works" in the fourteenth century, it is William Caxton and his contemporaries who first produced in "England

the earliest critical utterances" in the late fifteenth century. A *Handbook on Literature*, ed. William Flint Thrall and Addison Hibbard, rev. ed. C. Hugh Holman (1936; New York: Odyssey Press, 1960), 116–18; Spurgeon, I, cxxx; Malone, 172; Tyrrwhit, quoted in *The Canterbury Tales*, ed. Thomas Wright, Percy Society 24, 25, 26, 3 Vols. (London: T. Richards, 1847) 24, xxiii–xxiv.

217. Legouis, *History*, 179–80.

218. Courthope, 304; Howard, *Idea*, 168; William Minto, *Characteristics of English Poets*, 2d. ed. (1874; London: William Blackwood and Sons, 1885), 39.

Malone sees the non-reality: "On an actual pilgrimage in fourteenth-century England this give and take would have been impossible: no innkeeper would have dreamt of behaving in this way towards a gentleman [in this case, the pilgrim Franklin], and if he did so behave no gentleman would have put up with it." Malone, as always, sees "humorous purposes." (192–93)

219. Courthope, 304.

220. Courthope, 289; Keen, 5. Speirs gives only fleeting references to the Host.

221. Baldwin, 76; "The wordes moote be cosyn to the dede." (A742); "If men shal telle proprely a thyng, / The word moost cosyn be to the werkyng." (H209–10); "the wordis moot be cosynes to the thinges of whiche thei speken." (III, Pr. 12 end)

222. A748–50.

223. OED, s.v. "victual" sb. 4. "1558 Br. Watson *Sev. Sacram.* ix. 50. This heauenly foode is..a strong vitale, making vs able to endure the painful iorney to the kingdome of heauen."; "A better fode may na man fynde, / For to lastand lyf it will vs lede." (Brown, No. 48, 31–32)

I do not subscribe to the idea that "vitaille" is the *necessary* word because it fits the meter of the line and "fode" does not; the poet planned the line—as well as the word.

224.　　　　A semely man Oure Hooste was withalle
　　　　　　For to been a marchal in an halle.
　　　　　　A large man he was with eyen stepe—
　　　　　　A fairer burgeys was ther noon in Chepe—
　　　　　　Boold of his speche, and wys, and wel ytaught,
　　　　　　And of manhod hym lakkede right naught.

Eek therto he was right a myrie man.

(A751–57)

225. Malone 159; "And wonder semli was wit-al" *Cursor Mundi*, 18830.

226. *A Fifteenth-Century Courtesy Book*, ed. R. W. Chambers, EETS o.s. 148 (London; Oxford University Press, 1914; reprint, 1962), 12, 15.

227. "God hath so ordeynyd in his halle." (10966); MED, s.v. "hal(le," n. 1b. Fig.: *Pr. of Consc.* 8098 "Loverd! better es a day lastand / In þi halles þan a thowsand; / Þat es, better es in heven a day, / Þan a thowsand here þat passes oway."; *Exeter* I, Christ, Nativity, (4); "I ordeyn… / In hevyn an halle for mannys sake." (56–57)

228. MED, s.v. "stepe"; OED, s.v. "steep." The modern version of the *Canterbury Tales* according to David Wright replaces "stepe" with "protruding," thereby eliminating all other possibilities.

229.
    Þe leouns whelpe whenne hit is born
    Liþ deed til þe þridde morn
    wiþouten lif of any lym
    His fadir þenne comeþ to him
    And wiþ his cry þat is so grise
    He ȝueþ his whelpe lif to rise
    So dud ihesu oure champioun
    Þo he lay deed for oure raunsoun
    whenne his fadir wolde he made
    Him vp to rise vs alle to glade
    Of leoun also þe kynde is heȝe
    Slepyng loukeþ he neuer his eȝe
    Nor ihesus þouȝe he his goost ȝalde.

(18645–57)

See also *"Natura leonis," Physiologus*, p. 3.

230. One of the windows in the cathedral at Le Mans illustrates this roaring lion as a figure of the Resurrection. See Charles Rufus Morey, *Mediaeval Art* (New York: W. W. Norton, 1942), 268 and fig. 100; "The eyen of the juge that seeth and demeth alle thinges." p. 384 (V, pr. 6, 310)

231. See n. 199 above.

232. OED, s.v. "fair"; MED, s.v. "fair."; "For certes Jhesu Crist is entierly al good; in hym nys noon imperfeccioun." (I 1005–10)
The noun *fair* can be eqivalent to *Jesus*. See "?Rolle, *Luf es lyf* 81," cited in MED.

233.
Into þe scole she (Mary) coom goonde
And greet gederynge þer in fonde
Of wise maistris of þat lawe
Wiþ hem sittynge ihesu she sawe
þe beste maistris of þat toun
He ȝaf hem alle redi resoun.

(12615–20)

234. "Seuen poyntes of cristes manhede," (p. 26 ff.); "in bodi and in saule" (p. 28). See, for example, "Docetism."

235. "The first [point] is, that Iesu crist, goddes sone of heuen, / Was sothefastely consayued of the maiden mari, / And toke flesh and blode, and bicome man." p. 26 (120–22)
After stating the Host lacked nothing of manhood, the next line reads: "Eek thereto he was right a myrie man." The word *right* carries the strength of "genuinely, truly, legitimately" in regard to manhood, both here and in the line before it. In addition, *thereto* can mean "accordingly," or, when referring to a desired end, it can say, "for that purpose." And, finally, when related to doctrine, *thereto* intends testifying "to the truth of." With all these considerations, the two lines can confirm that, "He had all the attributes of a man, and legitimately he was a man belonging to Mary," or "…testifying to the truth of [his manhood] he was truly a man of Mary."

236. "Thurgh might and strenth of the haligast." p. 26 (123); "my *fader soule* that is *deed*." (A781) Italics added.

237. Kolve, *Imagery*, 2.

238. B. Page, 3.

239. The Risen Christ's appearance to Mary Magdalen:

In hevyn to ordeyn ȝow A place
to my ffadyr now wyl I go
to merth and joye and grett solace
And endeles blys to brynge ȝow to.

(50–53)

240. Keen, 11; Baldwin, 79, 87–88: "Hu murie hit were, to have the siht off godes face"; B. Page, 2; Delasanta, "Penance," 243. (Bible passage quoted is actually Luke 14:15); *Ludus Coventriæ*: "now xal we dwellyn in blysful place / In joye and endeles myrthe." (1354–55)

241. Baldwin, 62; "spak of myrthe amonges othere thynges, / Whan that we hadde maad our rekenynges." (A759–60); "And of a myrthe I am right now bythoght, / To doon yow ese, and it shal coste noght." (A767–68); "Crist hadde boght us with his blood." (C501)

242. "But ye be myrie, I wol yeve yow myn heed!" (A782)

243. MED, s.v. "mistik(e" n.

> Cryst and hijs membrys, men,
> O (one) body beþe ine mystyke.
>
> (23/630–31)

244. *Oweth* al his lif to God as longe as he hath lyved, and eek as longe as he shal lyve, that no goodnesse ne hath to *paye* with his *dette* to God to whom he *oweth* al his lyf./ For trust wel, "he shal *yeven acountes*," as seith Seint Bernard, "of alle the goodes that han be yeven hym in this present lyf, and how he hath hem *despended*;/ in so muche that ther shal nat perisse an heer of his heed, ne a moment of an houre ne shal nat perisse of his tyme, that he ne shal *yeve of it a rekenyng*. (I 250–55) Italics added.

245. "And al this shal be doon in thy presence; / I wol noght speke out of thyn audience." (E328–29); MED, s.v. "audience."

246.
> And therfore wol I maken yow disport,
> As I seyde erst, and doon yow som confort.
> And if yow liketh alle by oon assent
> For to stonden at my juggement,
> And for to werken as I shal yow seye,
> To-morwe, whan ye riden by the weye,
>
> .   .   .
>
> Hoold up youre hondes, withouten moore speche.
>
> (A775–83)
>
> Oure conseil was nat longe for to seche.
> Us thoughte it was noght worth to make it wys,
> And graunted hym withouten moore avys,

And bad him seye his voirdit as hym leste.

(A784–87)

247. Keen, 16; Malone, 194. A reviewer, trying to discover *psychological motivations* for the Host's actions, sees him as an opportunist and "unclear what law governs him." (B. Page, 12) If we grant that the Host is Christ, then Chaucer is demonstrating that the Host is a law unto himself.

248. "Tel me anon withouten wordes mo." (A808); "alwey a man shal putten his wyl to be subget to the wille of God." (I 1045)

249. MED, s.v. "solas"; Walter Skeat, *The Complete Works of Geoffrey Chaucer*, 2d ed., 7 vols, (1894-1987; Oxford, The Clarendon Press, 1900), V, 58, n. 798, "Tales best suited to instruct and amuse."; Baugh, Glossary, "entertainment"; Andrew Ingraham, ed., *Geoffrey Chaucer's The Prologue to the Book of the Tales of Canterbury* (New York: Macmillan, 1922) Glossary, "amusement, entertainment"; D. Wright, 21, "The most amusing and instructive tale." This last example also replaces Chaucer's plural *tales* with the singular, *tale*.

250. Delasanta, "Judgment," 299; Howard, *Idea*, 157; "whilom han bifalle." (A795)

251.
> This thyng was graunted, and oure othes swore
> With ful glad herte, and preyden hym also
> That he wolde vouchesauf for to do so,
> And that he wolde been oure governour,
> And of our tales juge...

(A810–14)

252.
> Lord & god he shal be oure
> And euermore *oure gouernoure*.

(18365–66. Italics added)

> For he ys *our governour* ever.

(*Stanzaic Life*, 4359. Italics added)

Baldwin, 64; "Now Jhesu Crist... / ...governe us in his grace." (B1160–61); "God governeth alle the thinges of the world...; and seidest that alle thinges wolen obeyen to hym." (*Boethius*, III, Pr. 12, 170–80); "In goostly gladnesse to governe vs and guye." (*Minor Poems* I, "A Procession of *Corpus Cristi*," 35, l. 3)

253. Weightiness is also demonstrated in the word *shape*, generally understood as *prepare*. When the Host proposes that he judge, and ride with the pilgrims, he concludes,

> And if ye vouchesauf that it be so,
> Tel me anon withouten wordes mo,
> And I wol erly shape me therfore.
>
> (A808–09)

Shape, when said of Christ, indicates the plan of his passion for God's purpose. The MED ("shapen," 3b) gives two noteworthy examples: A Wyclif sermon speaks of how Christ "shope his passioun to answere to byggynge [bygynnynge, *source*] of mannys synne"; a parable from *Cursor Mundi* describes, "To oon mote we all concent / And sithen shape þe Iugement." (9713–14). So, in addition to meaning *prepare*, *shape* can indicate God's decree, or his ordaining that something should occur. Then for Christ to "erly shape" himself would indicate his plan to be mankind's judge from the beginning.

254. Chester, II, Last Judgment, 431, (l. 110); Herry Lovelich, *History of the Holy Grail*, ed. Frederick J. Furnivall, EETS e.s. 20. 24, 28, 30, 95 (London: Kegan Paul, Trench, Trübner and Co., 1874–1905) I, 51: 43–50: "My synnes to Repotten"; Manly, *Canterbury Tales*, 539, n. to 814; Kennedy, 152; Wyclif, 1389, "Nyle ʒe gesse, that I am to accusinge ʒou anemptis the fadir," John 5:45 in *The Gospels: Gothic, Anglo-Saxon, Wycliffe, and Tyndale Versions*, 4th ed. (London: Gibbings, 1907); 1John 2:1; Mirk, "our trew avoket euermor" (153); Luke 23:34; Delasanta also draws attention to the Trinitarian possibilities of "my fader soule" and the Host referred to as "lordly as a kyng." ("Judgment," 300, n. 6); "soper at *oure* aller cost." (A799) Italics added.

255. Manly, *Canterbury Tales*, n. to 791, p. 593, draws attention to the use of *our* cost, rather than *your* cost. When the Host says "our," he has not yet made himself part of the pilgrim group, so *our* could indicate that he is part of *another group*, as well. The Trinity is a possible interpretation. In the Towneley Play of the Annunciation, God says, "Ryghtwysnes wyll *we* make." p. 86 (29)

256. Rubin has determined that Biblical "tensions…were resolved in the eucharist in the creation of a symbol which bound the essential narratives of incarnation, crucifixion, and the legacy of redemption." (348) Within the introduction of his Host, in the

General Prologue, Chaucer has brought together, in a covert fashion, references to the birth, death, and the redemptive promise associated with Christ. In this very mystical aspect, Chaucer's *Host* holds the Christic identity of the Eucharistic *Host* once again.

257. "Goon by the weye" (A771); "riden by the weye" (A780); Robinson, 668; OED, s.v. "way"; Gardiner, 22.

258. Guide—B245; B1449; D1643; G45; F866. Lead—*Boethius*, V, Pr. 1, 40–50; *Romance of the Rose*, 7225; Baldwin, 61; Gardiner, 131.
    Reginald Pecock, in 1443, uses much of the terminology we have seen Chaucer associate (in the *General Prologue*) with Our Host. Pecock, however, is speaking of Christ. In Chapter 12 he tells of God who is "*gouernor* of alle creaturis" (48) and of His "gouernauncis" in Chapter 21 (218–219). In Chapter 22 (219–220) he describes Christ as "oure *foode*...oure euen *wey goer wiþ vs in pilgrimage* toward heuenly jerusalem,...our *price paied* for oure raunsoun... þou art *afore þi fadir oure aduoker*... oure *reuler*...[and] *reward.*" *Reule of Crysten Religioun*, EETS o.s. 171 (London: Oxford University Press, 1927). (Italics added.)

259. One source for the homily is the introductory pages of *"Come to Me" in the Blessed Sacrament*, published by Apostolate for Perpetual Adoration, Box 46502, Mt. Clemens, Michigan.

260. Rubin explains that many images related to the Eucharist merged. In works of art: the Last Supper and the Consecration of the Mass became paired (298–302). Correspondences were found in the Incarnation, Passion, and Eucharist in the Easter Week liturgies (142). Fraternities dedicated to the Eucharist at Corpus Christi often were special participants in the Easter sepulchre ceremonies (236–37). These ceremonies were common in England; their purpose was to encourage recollections of Christ's burial and resurrection (294–96), rather as a parallel to the Christmas crèche.

261. "For trewely, confort ne myrthe is noon / To ride by the weye doumb as a stoon." (A773–74); Craig, 134, 133. Italics added to Chaucer and Craig.

262.   A-morwe, whan that day bigan to sprynge,
                Up roos oure Hoost, and was oure aller cok,
                And gadrede us togidre alle in a flok,
                And forth we riden a litel moore than paas

Unto the wateryng of Seint Thomas;
And there oure Hoost bigan his hors areste.

(A822–27)

263. Rubin, 55.

264. Wickham elaborates "the first stage used as a street theatre in the present context was the water conduit in Cheapside.… After 1377, however, several other conduits and similar monuments were built in London and taken into service as street theatres for ceremonial processions almost as soon as they were built." (I, p. 58); D. W. Robertson, Jr., *Chaucer's London* (New York: John Wiley and Sons, 1968; reprint, Ann Arbor, MI: UMI, 1992), 38–39.

265. Skeat, *The Complete Works,* 5: 59, n. 826.

266. OED, s.v. "water," sb 2.

267. Rubin, 191–93. Rubin also describes how symbolically important processions became in association with the Eucharist. (207) Aquinas' well-known *Pange, Lingua* was eminently suitable for use in these ceremonies. (246)

268. Emile Mâle, *The Gothic Image*, trans. Dora Nussey (New York: E. P. Dutton, 1913; reprint, New York: Harper Torchbook, 1958). Mâle explains in Chapter IV how one idea can have two, three, or four interpretations on different levels. Fletcher offers a similar thought. (73)

269. OED, s.v. "God" 13; MED, s.v. "cok," "A veiled variant of god"; OED, s.v. "cock" sb 8, "perversion of the word God,"; Chester II, the Passion:

> Men, for Cockes face!
> how longe shall poydrace*
> stand naked in this place?
> goe, neyles him to the Tree!
>
> p. 303 (533–36)

*Derogatory epithet, *dusty, dirty*. MED, s.v. "peudras"; Chaucer, (H9), (I 29).

270. OED, s.v. "flock," 4 fig. "In a spiritual sense the whole body of Christians, in relation to Christ as the 'Chief Shepherd'"; "Almyghty Lord, o Jhesu Crist... / ... hierde of us alle." (G191–92) Acting out of the epithets was a technique used by medieval dramatists as was noted above in Chapter IV, p.46.

271. Rubin, 226–27.

272. Donaldson, 948; *Boethius*, "God ledeth and constreyneth alle thingis" (V, Pr. 1, 40–50); Rose, 344.

273. *Divine Office*, II

> *Te, trina Deitas, unaque poscimus:*
> *Sic nos tu visita, sicut te colimus;*
> *Per tuas semitas duc nos quo tendimus,*
> *Ad lucem quam inhabitas.*

(1460–61)

At York a pilgrim prays, "lord who has lent me this life for to lead, / In my ways mayst thou guide me thus wandering alone." (p. 328)

274. Jonathan Keates and Angelo Hornak, *Canterbury Cathedral* (London: Summerfield Press, 1980; reprint, London: Scala Publications, 1991), 9; Swann, 15, 51; Hans Jantzen, *The High Gothic: The Classic Cathedrals of Chartres, Reims, Amiens*, trans. James Palmes (Hamburg: Rowohlt Taschenbuch, 1957; reprint, Minerva Press, 1962), 178.

275.
> And Jhesu, for his grace, wit me sende
> To shewe yow the wey, in this viage,
> Of thilke parfit glorious pilgrymage
> That highte Jerusalem celestial.

(I 48–51)

Baldwin, 89–90.

276. Lumiansky, *Sondry*, 27.

277. "For Goddes digne passioun" (B1175); "by the croys which that Seint Eleyne fond." (C951)

278. "Goddes mercy!" (E2419); "God yow blesse." (E1240); "by Seint Austyn!" (B1631); "by my savacioun." (H58)

279. "Tel on, a devel wey!" (A3134, A3137); "God yeve thee sorwe!" (H15, H17)

280. "Dun is in the myre!" (H5); "Straw for youre gentillesse!" (F695)

281. "'Harrow!' quod he, 'by nayles and by blood!'" (C288); Baugh, p. 489; "This was a fals cherl and a fals justise." (C289); *Cursor Mundi* : "Þenne brast þo brasen ȝates strong / And stelen lokes

þat þere on hong / ... / þenne þei shulde be mery & glad / þe folke þat in wo were stad." (18103–10)

Harrow can also be heard from the receiving end of the harrowing. At Towneley, for example, Beelzebub (in hell) bemoans his fate:

> harro! oure yates begyn to crak!
> In sonder, I trow, they go,
> And hell, I trow, will all to-shak;
> Alas, what I am wo!
>
> XXV, p. 300 (209–12)

282. "Pees! and that anon!" (D850); "Pees, namoore of this!" (D1298); "Pees!" (D1334), (D1762).

283. The suggested alternate expressions were used elsewhere by Chaucer: (D1031), (G927), (B2405–10), (H37). Biblical references: Phil 4:9, 1Thes 5:23, 2Thes 3:16, Heb 13:20; Chester II, XVIII: "I am very prince of peace" (162); Towneley, XXV, addressing the devil: "A prynce of peasse shall enter therat / wheder ye will or none." (195–96)

284.
> For certeinly, as that thise clerkes seyn,
> Whereas a man may have noon audience,
> Noght helpeth it to tellen his sentence.
> And wel I woot the substance is in me,
> If any thyng shal wel reported be.
>
> (B3990–94)

Note to B3993.

285. *Substance* 1; "He his God, of þe substaunce of þe fader biȝeten tofore þe worldes." (29.195); *Boethius*, III, Pr. 12, 170–80: "good is the substaunce of God and of blisfulnesse."; MED, s.v. "substaunce" 1 (b).

286. *In ipso namque panis et vinum in Christi corpus et sanguinem* substantialiter *convertuntur. Divine Office*, p. 1470.

OED, s.v. "accident": II. 6. "*Logic.* A property or quality not essential to our conception of a substance; an attribute. Applied especially in Scholastic Theology to the material qualities remaining in the sacramental bread...; the essence being alleged to be changed, though the accidents remained the same."

Though *substance* also intends essence of the nature of the Trinity, in this case we understand "the Incarnate Christ," because the Host is speaking of himself, in particular.

287. (A4345); (A4358).

288. Manly, *New Light*, 78 ff. The fourteenth-century innkeeper's wife was named Christian.

289. MED, s.v. "herien" v. (1); Brown, No. 125: "Holi fadur, y herie þe" (34); Brown, No. 14: "Al þat ys in heuene þe heryȝeth" (5); Brown, No. 13: "A god, þe heyȝe trinite, / Alle gostes heryȝe þe!" (25–26); "God they thanke and herye" (E616); "[He] herieth Crist that is of hevene kyng." (B1808)

290. MED, s.v. "herien" v. (2); "Til þat our lauerd harid hell" (1446); "the godhede went untill hell, And heried it" (fourth point of Christ's manhood, p. 28); "How he suld hery hell" (1535); "hym that harwed helle." (A3512)

291. S.v. "heraud." See *Oxford Dictionary of English Christian Names*, ed. E. G. Withycombe, 2d rev. ed. (Oxford: Clarendon Press, 1963), s.v. "Harold."

292. MED, s.v. "bailli(e"; "bail(le." OED, s.v. "baillie": (1305) *Fall and the Passion* 22 "God ȝaf him a gret maistre…of paradis al þe balye." Towneley XXII, "Thou art here in oure baly" (146); Rose, 378. Towneley XXV, "In that bayll ay shall thou be, / where sorowes seyr shall neuer sesse." (307–08); Rose, 455.

Malone comments on the similarity of the Host's name to that of the medieval innkeeper: "Evidence is wholly wanting that Chaucer's Harry Bailly had anything in common with the Harry Bailly of flesh and blood other than name, habitat, and occupation, three features not without importance but essentially *external*." (187, italics added.) I find this noteworthy because it acknowledges Chaucer's skillful use of externals, the *accidents* with which he cloaks the substance, the concealed essence of Our Host.

293. Many who write about the Host will choose to refer to him as "Herry" (or even "Harry"), no doubt to add variety to the necessary vocabulary. This, however, works at odds with Chaucer's *sentence*. The idea is to nag at readers with the word *Host*. Some would understand; for the rest of his audience his excuse for the repetition could be lack of imagination. The "monotonous repetition" has a job to do—the poem is waving another flag.

294.   I rede that oure Hoost heere shal bigynne,
              For he is moost envoluped in synne.

                                                (C941–42)

295. *Harrowing of Hell*

              Sunne (sin) fond þou neuer non
              In me as in oþer mon.

                                     p. 9 (75–76)

Douay-Rheims, Isa. 53:6; "Jhesu Crist took upon hymself the peyne of alle oure wikkednesses." (I 280–85); "Jhesu Crist is entierly al good; in hym nys noon imperfeccioun." (I 1005–10)

296. Volume 5 of his edition of *The Canterbury Tales*, p. 173, n. to (B1625); p. 268, n. to (C314).

297. John Wyclif, *Selected English Works*, ed. Thomas Arnold, 3 Vols. (Oxford: Clarendon Press, 1869–71), 1, CXI, 376.

298. Middle English *bon* or *bone*, in addition to *good*, also carries the significance of *gift*, *prayer*, *command*, and *reward*, as well as the obvious *bones of the body*.

299. "God hymself is sovereyn good." (*Boethius*, III, Pr. 12, 160–70)

300. Kolve, *Imagery*, 285; B. Page, 8; Delasanta, "Penance," 245.

301. "Now comth hasardrie with…mysspendynge of tyme" (I 790–95); "For trust wel, 'he shal yeven acountes,' as seith Seint Bernard, 'of alle the goodes that han be yeven hym in this present lyf…ne a moment of an houre ne shal nat perisse of his tyme, that he ne shal yeve of it a rekenyng.'" (I 250–55)

    Christ's words from *Cursor Mundi* express a similar concern about using time fruitfully as the day ends.

              Mi fadir werkes mot I do
              Whil þat I haue day þerto
              For now [b]ihoueþ þe son to spede
              For to do his fadir dede
              Worche he most bifore þe niȝt
              Whiles þe day lesteþ liȝt

                                    (13536–41)

302.   But taak it nought, I prey yow, in desdeyn.
              This is the poynt, to speken short and pleyn,
              That ech of yow, to shorte with oure weye,

> In this viage shal telle tales tweye
> To Caunterbury-ward, I mene it so,
> And homward he shal tellen othere two
>
> (A789–94)

303.
> Lordynges everichoon,
> Now lakketh us no tales mo than oon.
> Fulfilled is my sentence and my decree.
>
> (I 15–17)

Baldwin, 63–64; Gardner, 14.

304. Jackson quotes the description of a northern European spring-time from an enthusiastic Helen Waddell: "Spring comes slowly up that way, but when it comes it is an ecstasy. In the North, far more than in the South, Persephone comes actually from the dead." (225)

305.
> By processe off tymë long,
> Thow shalt *retourne ageyn* by grace
> Vn-to thyn ownë duë place,
> Reste in god, and ther abyde.
>
> (12406–09. Italics added.)

> And in thy way, haue in mynde;
> Epicicles thow shalt ffynde,
> Off Infortunyes fful dyuers,
> Off sodeyn caas, fful peruers;
> ffor *thy lyff* (yt ys no doute,)
> *Ys lyk a cercle* that goth aboute,
> Round and swyfft as any thouht,
> Wych in hys course ne cesset nouht
> Yiff he go ryht, and wel compace
> Tyl he kome to hys restyng place,
> Wych ys in god, yiff he wel go
> Hys ownë place wych he kam ffro.
>
> (12373–84. Italics added.)

306. Craig, 135. Withington, in *English Pageantry*, describes a Corpus Christi procession in which some of the actors participated in Coventry in the fifteenth century. It "took place in the morning: the order of companies was from the youngest to the oldest. The members of each rode, and their journeymen walked. The members were preceded by their torchbearers; the religious bodies followed the laity; the Trinity Guild bore the Host, which was

attended by priests, and the fraternity of the Corpus Christi Guild did special honor to the solemnity.

"The Mayor and the Aldermen with their attendants, and the civil and religious fraternities, and all the ecclesiastics of the city would join in the procession. *Sometimes Herod, and perhaps the chief persons in the other craft plays, rode in it.*" (I:23. Italics added.) Robert Withington, *English Pageantry: An Historical Outline*, 2 Vols. (Cambridge, MA: Harvard University Press, 1918–20; reprint, New York: Benjamin Blom, 1963).

307. "The cercle of the daies [which] folewith the cercle of the names of the monthes." (Part I, no. 10) This does not allow for the discrepancy in the calendar; that is another matter.

"From oon Estre day unto another Estre day." (I 550–55)

Basically, Easter occurs on the first Sunday after the full moon following the vernal equinox—unless the full moon occurs on Sunday. In that case Easter is celebrated the following Sunday and can vary from March 22 to April 25. But if you consider the Jewish holiday of Passover in conjunction with the computation, and consider that the Jewish calendar has a different basis—the date arrived at could be quite different. (See "Paschal controversy," *Britannica*.) Nowadays the computation is done for us and we don't think about it—but even today Eastern portions of the Christian church often celebrate on a different date from the West.

308. *Festivals*, p. 220 (303–06); "Aught forto resceyve [the Eucharist] anes in the yhere, / That is at sai, at paskes." p. 66 (320–21)

The pattern recounted in the *General Prologue* since the Host came on the scene can also be followed as a progression of Holy Week: the first meal as the Lord's Supper (Holy Thursday), the offering of his head and his own cost (Good Friday), the night that follows (the entombment) and then he "rose up" (Easter, the Resurrection).

As the departure day began, it was not the sun that was noted rising, but it was Our Host who rose up. Resurrection is a rising up. There are instances in medieval dramas which juxtapose the two ideas last noted: the Resurrection, followed by Christ waking mankind, all of whom are pilgrims of course. In both cases the lines below were preceded by a stage direction indicating *Iesus Resurgens*:

Earthly man, that I haue wrought
awake out of thy sleepe!

Chester II, XVIII (155–56)

Earthly man, that I haue wroght,
wightly wake, and slepe thou noght!

Towneley, XXVI (226–27)

309. "Heere in this place, sittynge by this post." (A800)

310. Baldwin, 56, 74; Howard, *Idea*, 165–68.

311. Howard, *Writers*, 11. Italics added.
Chaucer's wording (again) is of interest:

To Caunterbury-ward, I mene it so,
And homward...

The poet says "home," not London, not Chcpc. To remove the
interruption, "I mene it so," we have "toward Canterbury the Ce-
lestial City, and home." This puts me in mind of the wishful
thought on a strenuous journey—a desire to head for the farm
(or Texas, or Denver, or the South Side, etc.) and home. The ex-
pression can be seen as a simple longing for *home*, ultimately
meaning *Heaven*, a very Augustinian sentiment. Augustine sees
pilgrims hungering, thirsting, and longing for their eternal home.
See *A Companion to the Study of St. Augustine*, ed. Roy W.
Battenhouse (New York: Oxford University Press, 1955), 412.

This also lends itself to the circular path of time: as they con-
tinue in the same direction that they are going, in the end, they
will return *home*.

312. Only time and hard work will tell if each tale has a second mean-
ing. Delasanta, for example, notes details concerned with the
Host's role similar to the biblical Servant-Master, as well as ele-
ments of Judgment and the eschatological supper; he feels they
are used satirically by Chaucer. But what if all these ideas that
have been perceived were not meant as *satire?*

Just one more example we might think about comes from
Edgar Duncan. He did a detailed study of treatises on medieval
alchemy, translating several works from Latin to make proper
comparisons to Chaucer's use of such works. ("The Literature of
Alchemy and Chaucer's Canon's Yeoman's Tale: Framework,
Theme, and Characters" *Speculum* 43 [Oct 1968]: 633–56) He
found that "Chaucer, the dramatic artist, is so arranging the quo-

tations from the treatises to make them say what he wants them to say." (653) Chaucer made "subtle changes in the emphasis." (654) Duncan wonders if Chaucer has managed affairs so that his *pilgrim* "speaks one message…[and] *Chaucer* speaks at the same time quite another message." (656. Italics added.) This is the degree of cleverness I have come to expect from our poet.

313. Those who are familiar with the *Canterbury Tales* know that some of the pilgrims, after they are introduced in the *General Prologue*, are never mentioned again or heard from. There is an explanation for this apparent author-negligence; the explanation is in harmony with the foregoing proposals, but it is beyond this project.

314. Manly describes a tabard richly embroidered "with armorial bearings," in the notes to his *Canterbury Tales* (p. 497, n. to l. 20) and says they can still be seen today. Similar examples noted in the MED and OED are all late fifteenth century, and seem to be associated with a later development; "The hye God, on whom that we bileeve, / In wilful poverte chees to lyve his lyf." (D1178–79); "pore paraille and pylgrymes wedes," in *The Vision of Piers the Plowman*, ed. Walter W. Skeat, EETS o.s. 28, 38 54, 67, 81 (London: N. Trübner and Co., 1869), II:180 (l. 228); Chester II, XIX, stage direction indicates, "*Tunc veniet Ihesus in habitu peregrinæ.*" (p. 353, follows l. 32) In the Towneley play (XXVII), Lucas assumes from Christ's appearance "Thou art a pilgreme, as we ar." p. 333 (269)

    The entry from *Gesta Romanorum*, mentioned in the previous chapter, also finds Christ himself noting that he is clad "as a seruaunte" and declares he had wished for "nought but to vtterly vtilite and necessite; I sought no thing in the worlde but alonly mesurably lyvelode and clothing." (See n. 210, above.) His words represent an aspect of the times. Gospel, or Evangelical, poverty was of great importance. St. Francis of Assisi took this as a guide for his life, and that of his followers. See also *Waldensians, Poor Lombards, Poor of Lyons, Beguines.*

315. OED, s.v., "mystery"; see n. 243, above.

316.   I

        The lord þat is a howsholder,
           With faire festis folk he fat;
        ȝiueþ hem wedys (clothes) hym self doþe were,
           On bolstre bed her balys bat;

With hym on bedde, man, þou sat
    On þe bolstre of heuene blisse.
With hys fleisshe he fediþ þe, þou wost wel þis,
þi sowle schal be clad as hys
    In lyfe þat neuermore lat.

II

He seiþ þat god is sooþfast sunne,
    And in þat same þi sowle is clad;
þi lordes wede (garment) þan hast þou wonne

p. 210 (3–20)

317. *S and A* includes an excerpt from the *Anticlaudianus* of Alanus de
Insulis (d. 1202) as a source for *The Second Nun's Tale*. The mar-
ginal gloss translates two of the lines to say that in Mary's womb
"the Son wove for himself the vestment of our salvation." (667)
The garment of Christ had a spiritual significance in the Middle
Ages that is no longer in our thought patterns.

318. Fletcher, 307.

319. Baldwin (quotes de Lubac), 39. Quoted earlier on p. 72, above.

320. I'm sure he had good reasons for omitting the warrior character-
istics. It may have been too obvious a clue, or too difficult to as-
similate with the rest of the Host's qualities; (D1660–62).

321. Brown, No. 36:

I come vram þe wedlok as a svete spouse,
    þet habbe my wif wiþ me in-nome.
I come vram viȝt a stalworþe knyȝt,
    þet myne vo habbe ouercome.
I come vram þe chepyng as a Riche chapman,*
    þet mankynde habbe ibouȝt.
I Come vram an vncouþe londe as a sely pylegrym,
    þet ferr habbe i-souȝt.

(5–8)

*In contrast, the *chapman* of hell is the Devil, who also bargains
for souls. (MED, s.v. "chapman.")

IX: A Conclusion

322. Delasanta, "Penance," 246; Delasanta, "Judgment," 299.

323. P. 147.

324. P. 179, *History*. Italics added.

325. Matthew 11:29; John 1:29, 1:36.

326. Spurgeon I, Webbe, in his *Discourse on English Poetrie* (1586): "For such was his bolde spyrit, that what enormities he saw...he would not spare...eyther in playne words, or els in some prety and pleasant couert." (p. 129).

327.
>By Goddes bones! Whan I bete my knaves,
>She bryngeth me forth the grete clobbed staves,
>And crieth, "Slee the dogges everichoon,
>And brek hem, bothe bak and every boon!"
> And if that any neighebore of myne
>Wol nat in chirche to my wyf enclyne,
>Or be so hardy to hire to trespace,
>Whan she comth hoom she rampeth in my face,
>And crieth, "False coward, wrek thy wyf!
>By corpus bones, I wol have thy knyf,
>And thou shalt have my distaf and go spynne!"
>Fro day to nyght right thus she wol bigynne.
>"Allas!" she seith, "that evere I was shape
>To wedden a milksop, or a coward ape,
>That wol been overlad with every wight!
>Thou darst nat standen by thy wyves right!"
> This is my lif, but if that I wol fighte;
>And out at dore anon I moot me dighte,
>Or elles I am but lost, but if that I
>Be lik a wilde leoun, fool-hardy.
>I woot wel she wol do me slee som day
>Som neighebore, and thanne go my way;
>For I am perilous with knyf in honde,
>Al be it that I dar nat hire withstonde,
>For she is byg in armes, by my feith:
>That shal he fynde that hire mysdooth or seith,—
>But lat us passe awey fro this mateere.

>(B3087–113)

328.   But doutelees, as trewe as any steel
            I have a wyf, though that she povre be,
            But of hir tonge, a labbynge shrewe is she,
            And yet she hath an heep of vices mo;
            Therof no fors! lat alle swiche thynges go.
            But wyte ye what? In conseil be it seyd
            Me reweth soore I am unto hire teyd.
            For, and I sholde rekenen every vice
            Which that she hath, ywis I were to nyce;
            And cause why, it sholde reported be
            And toold to hire of somme of this meynee,—
            Of whom, it nedeth nat for to declare,
            Syn wommen konnen outen swich chaffare;
            And eek my wit suffiseth nat therto,
            To tellen al, wherfore my tale is do.

                                        (E2426–440)

329. *Britannica*, s.v. "Inquisition." It was Bernard of Clairvaux' opinion that: "Faith must be the result of conviction and should not be imposed by force [*Fides suadenda, non imponenda*]. Heretics are to be overcome by arguments, not by arms."

330. Pp. 315, 118.

331. See n. 39 above, for prevalence of thought regarding an imminent change to come in the Church.

332. Kolve, *Corpus Christi*, 192 ff. Another demonstration of religious imaging far from twentieth-century mental pictures is an illustration of a cathedral window in Swann's book (p. 147) where Christ as Judge is represented with the two-edged sword of justice *clenched between his teeth.*

The sight of the crucified Christ brings dread to Satan and the devils try to flee His presence. (*Piers Plowman*, B, XVIII, ll. 283, 304–07)

In the *Meditations on the Life and Passion of Christ* (late thirteenth or early fourteenth century) the author has a different view of the nails of the Crucifixion. Assuming the hardness of a sinful heart, addressing Christ, he prays:

            for þouȝ myn herte be harde as stone,
            ȝite maiste þou gostly write þer-one
            Wiþe naylis and wiþ sper kene,
            And so schulen þe lettres be wel sene.

                                        p. 60 (5–8)

Comparable lines may also be found on page 36 of these *Medita-tions*. Ed. Charlotte D'Evelyn, EETS o.s. 158 (London: Oxford University Press, 1921)

333. *Confessio*, 5.40 "evermore / Him lacketh, that he hath inough" (II, p. 128); *Romance of the Rose*, "an userer, so God me se, / Shal nevere for richesse riche be, / But evermore pore and indigent" (Robinson, 5693–95); *Melibee*, "it is a greet shame to a man to have a povere herte and a riche purs." (Robinson, B2794); MED, s.v. "povre," fig.

334. Jackson, 21.

335. Keates, 35. To write or read of a pilgrimage is, in itself, a form of pilgrimage. As Gardiner explains:

"The Gregorian theme of pilgrimage defines the genre of biblical commentary in a very significant way: by bringing words to those for whom life has meaning in words.... The experience of reading a commentary is itself, in very radical literary ways, an enactment of the pilgrim life.... In this Easter Monday sermon...two dis-ciples and their journey [are] an allegory of "body and soul of each of Christ's faithful" at the time in any man's life when he faces an impasse in his labors to be found worthy of the heavenly achievement.... The heart, on its journey, like the disciples, meets the stranger and asks, 'Are you a pilgrim [stranger] in Jerusalem?'

"The words of this meditation-sermon...express [that] the in-dividual wayfarer's...'Jerusalem where deity is a stranger' is the 'heart of man who moves toward the vision of eternal peace.'...Emmaus...is but a moment in man's larger journey, the meeting-place where 'God and man approach each other, as God illumines [the heart] with his visitation, and man brings himself closer to deity through true love.'.... That vision of peace, that foretelling of the final arrival at the celestial Jerusalem, lasts but a moment...his imaginative response to Easter Monday has been guided by the double contents of the tradition—by scripture and by Gregory." (48–50)

Geoffrey Chaucer may have been inspired by this long tradition of verbal, and actual Easter Monday pilgrimages—as he planned for his pilgrims to set out "a litel moore than paas (Easter)."

BIBLIOGRAPHY

Altick, Richard D., *The Art of Literary Research* (New York: W. W. Norton, 1963).

Baldwin, Ralph, "The Unity of the Canterbury Tales," *Anglistica* 5 (Copenhagen: Rosenkilde and Baggar, 1955): 11–112.

Battenhouse, Roy W., ed. *A Companion to the Study of St. Augustine*, (New York: Oxford University Press, 1955).

Baum, Paull F., *Anglo-Saxon Riddles from the Exeter Book* (Durham, NC; Duke University Press, 1963).

Bennett, H. S., *Chaucer and the Fifteenth Century* (Oxford: Clarendon Press, 1947).

Bloomfield, Morton W., Piers Plowman *as a Fourteenth-century Apocalypse* (New Brunswick, NJ: Rutgers University Press, 1962).

Brewer, Derek Stanley, *Chaucer and His Time* (London: Thos. Nelson and Sons, 1963).

Bronson, Bertrand H., *In Search of Chaucer* (Toronto: University of Toronto Press, 1960).

Brown, Carleton, *Religious Lyrics of the Fourteenth Century*, (Oxford: Clarendon Press, 1924).

Bryan, W. F. and Germaine Dempster, ed., *Sources and Analogues of Chaucer's* Canterbury Tales (London: Routledge and Kegan Paul, 1941; reprint, New York: The Humanities Press, 1958).

The Cambridge History of English Literature I, A.W. Ward and A.R. Waller, eds. (Cambridge, England: Cambridge University Press, 1908).

Chambers, E. K., *The Medieval Stage*, 2 Vols. (London: Oxford University Press, 1903).

Chaucer, Geoffrey, ed. Albert C. Baugh, *Chaucer's Major Poetry* (New York: Appleton-Century-Crofts, 1963).

———, ed. F. N. Robinson, *The Works of Geoffrey Chaucer*, 2nd ed. (1933; Boston: Houghton Mifflin, 1961).

The Chester Plays, I, ed. Hermann Deimling, EETS e.s. 62 (London: Oxford University Press, 1892; reprint, 1926).

The Chester Plays, II, ed. Dr. Matthews, EETS e.s. 115 (London: Kegan Paul, Trench, Trübner and Co., 1916).

Chesterton, G. K., *Chaucer* (London: Faber and Faber, 1934).

Clark, Sydney A., *Cathedral France* (New York: Robert. M. McBride, 1931).

Clemen, Wolfgang, *Chaucer's Early Poetry* (New York: Barnes and Noble, 1964).

The Compact Edition of the Oxford English Dictionary: Complete Text Reproduced Micrographically, 2 Vols. (1884–1928; Oxford: Oxford University Press, 1971).

Courthope, W. J., *A History of English Poetry*, 6 Vols., 4th ed. (London: Macmillan,1895–1910; London: Macmillan, 1926).

Craig, Hardin, *English Religious Drama of the Middle Ages* (Oxford: Clarendon Press, 1955).

Cursor Mundi, ed. Richard Morris, EETS o.s. 57, 59, 62, 66, 68 (London: Kegan Paul, Trench, Trübner and Co., 1874-1878; reprint, London: Oxford University Press, 1966).

Curtius, Ernst Robert, *European Literature and the Latin Middle Ages*, trans. Willard R. Trask (1948; New York: Pantheon Books, 1953; reprint, New York: Harper Paperback, 1963).

Dahmus, Joseph, *William Courtenay: Archbishop of Canterbury 1381–1396* (University Park; Pennsylvania State University Press, 1966).

Delasanta, Rodney, "Penance and Poetry in the *Canterbury Tales*," *Speculum*, Vol. 93 (March 1978): 240-47.

——, "The Theme of Judgment in *The Canterbury Tales*," *MLQ* 31 (March 1970): 298-307.

Dillard, Annie, *The Writing Life* (New York: Harper and Row, 1989; New York: HarperPerennial, 1990).

Donaldson, E. T., ed., *Chaucer's Poetry: An Anthology for the Modern Reader* (New York: Ronald Press, 1958).

Duncan, Edgar H., "The Literature of Alchemy and Chaucer's

Canon's Yeoman's Tale: Framework, Theme, and Characters," *Speculum* 43 (Oct 1968): 633-656.

The Early English Version of Gesta Romanorum, ed. Sidney J. H. Herrtage, EETS e.s. 33 (London: Trübner and Co., 1879).

Encyclopædia Britannica, 1968 edition.

The Exeter Book I: An Anthology of Anglo-Saxon Poetry, ed. Israel Gollancz, EETS o.s. 104 (London: Kegan Paul, Trench, Trübner and Co., 1895).

Festivals of the Church, an appendix in *Legends of the Holy Rood*, ed. Richard Morris, EETS o.s. 46 (London: N. Trübner and Co., 1871).

A Fifteenth-Century Courtesy Book, ed. R. W. Chambers, EETS o.s. 148 (London; Oxford University Press, 1914; reprint, 1962).

Fitchen, John, *The Construction of Gothic Cathedrals : A Study of Medieval Vault Erection* (Oxford: Clarendon Press, 1961).

Fletcher, Angus, *Allegory: The Theory of a Symbolic Mode* (Ithaca, NY: Cornell University Press, 1964; Cornell Paperbacks, 1970).

Gardiner, F. C., *The Pilgrimage of Desire* (Leiden, Netherlands: E. J. Brill, 1971).

Gardner, John Champlin, *The Construction of Christian Poetry in Old English* (Carbondale, IL: Southern Illinois University Press, 1975).

Gayley, Charles Mills, *Plays of Our Forefathers* (New York: Duffield, 1907).

The Golden Legend of Jacobus de Voragine, trans. Granger Ryan and Helmut Ripperger (New York: Longmans, Green, 1941; reprint, Salem, NH: Ayer, 1987).

The Gospels: Gothic, Anglo-Saxon, Wycliffe and Tyndale Versions, ed. Joseph Bosworth and George Waring, 4th ed. (London: Gibbings, 1907).

Gower, John, ed. Reinhold Pauli, *Confessio Amantis of John Gower*, 3 Vols. (London: Bell and Daldy, 1857).

Hadow, Grace E., *Chaucer and His Times*, [Home University Library of Modern Knowledge No. 81] (New York: Henry Holt, [1914]).

A Handbook on Literature, ed. William Flint Thrall and Addison Hibbard, rev. ed. C. Hugh Holman (1936; New York: Odyssey Press, 1960).

The Hours of the Divine Office in English and Latin 3, 4 Vols. (Collegeville, MN: St. John's Abbey Press, 1963).

Howard, Donald R., *The Idea of the* Canterbury Tales (1976; Berkeley: University of California Press, 1978 paperback).

——, *Writers and Pilgrims: Medieval Pilgrimage Narratives and Their Posterity* (Los Angeles: University of California Press, 1980).

Huppé, Bernard F., *A Reading of the* Canterbury Tales, rev. ed. (1964; Albany, New York: State University of New York, 1967).

Ingraham, Andrew, ed., G*eoffrey Chaucer's The Prologue to the Book of the Tales of Canterbury* (New York: Macmillan, 1922).

Jackson, W. T. H., *The Literature of the Middle Ages* (New York: Columbia University Press, 1960).

Jantzen, Hans, *The High Gothic: The Classic Cathedrals of Chartres, Reims, Amiens*, trans. James Palmes (Hamburg: Rowohlt Taschenbuch, 1957; reprint, Minerva Press, 1962).

Keates, Jonathan and Angelo Hornak, *Canterbury Cathedral* (London: Summerfield Press, 1980; reprint, London: Scala Publications, 1991).

Keen, William, "'To Doon Yow Ese': a Study of the Host in the *General Prologue* of the *Canterbury Tales*," *Topic* 17 (1969): 5–18.

Kennedy, Charles W., trans., *Anthology of Old English Poetry* (New York: Oxford University Press, 1960).

Ker, William Paton, *English Literature: Medieval* [Home University Library of Modern Knowledge No. 45] (New York: Henry Holt, [1912]).

Kittredge, George Lyman, *Chaucer and His Poetry* (1915; reprint, Cambridge, MA: Harvard University Press, 1946).

Knight, Ione Kemp, ed., *Wimbledon's Sermon*: Redde Rationem Villicationis Tue [Duquesne Studies, Philological Series, No. 9.] (Pittsburgh, PA: Duquesne University Press, [1967]).

Kolve, V. A., *Chaucer and the Imagery of Narrative: the First Five Canterbury Tales* (Stanford, CA: Stanford University Press, 1984).

——, *The Play Called Corpus Christi* (Stanford, CA: Stanford University Press, 1966).

Langland, William, *The Vision of Piers the Plowman*, ed. Walter W. Skeat, EETS o.s. 28, 38 54, 67, 81 (London: N. Trübner and Co., 1869).

Lay Folks Catechism, ed. Thomas F. Simmons, EETS o.s. 118 (London: Henry E. Nolloth, 1901).

Lea, Henry Charles, *The Inquisition of the Middle Ages: Its Organization and Operation* [First published in 1887 as *The History of the Inquisition in the Middle Ages*. This edition constitutes Chapters VII–XIV of Vol. I] (London: Eyre and Spottiswoode, 1963; New York: Harper and Row, Harper Torchbooks, 1969).

Legends of the Holy Rood, ed. Richard Morris, EETS o.s. 46 (London: N. Trübner and Co. 1871).

Legouis, Emile, *A History of English Literature 650–1660*, trans. Helen Douglas Irvine, rev. ed., 2 Vols. (New York: Macmillan, 1929).

——, *Geoffrey Chaucer*, trans. L. Lailavoix (New York: E. P. Dutton, 1928).

Loomis, Roger S., "Was Chaucer a Laodicean?" in *Chaucer Criticism*: I: *The Canterbury Tales*, ed. Richard Schoeck and Jerome Taylor (Notre Dame, IN: University of Notre Dame Press, 1960).

Lounsbury, Thomas R., *Studies in Chaucer: His Life and Writings*, 3 Vols. (New York: Harper and Bro., 1892).

Lovelich, Herry, *History of the Holy Grail*, ed. Frederick J. Furnivall, EETS e.s. 20, 24, 28, 30 (London: Kegan Paul, Trench, Trübner and Co., 1874-1905).

Lowes, John Livingston, *Geoffrey Chaucer* (Boston: Houghton Mifflin, [1934]; Bloomington, IN: Indiana University Press, A Midland Book, 1958).

Ludus Coventriæ, ed. K. S. Block, EETS e.s. 120 (London: Oxford University Press, 1922).

Lumiansky, R. M., "Chaucer's *Canterbury Tales, Prologue*, 784-787," *Explicator* Vol. 5, No.3 (Dec 1946), No. 20.

——, *Of Sondry Folk* (Austin: University of Texas Press, 1955).

Lydgate, John, *Assembly of Gods*, ed. Oscar Lovell Triggs, EETS e.s.

69 (London: Oxford University Press, 1896).

———, *The Minor Poems of John Lydgate I*, ed. Henry Noble MacCracken, EETS e.s. 107 (London: Kegan Paul, Trench, Trübner and Co., 1911).

———, *The Pilgrimage of the Life of Man*, ed. Frederick J. Furnivall, EETS e.s. 77, 83, 92 (London: Kegan Paul, Trench, Trübner and Co., 1899, 1901, 1904).

Mack, Maynard, Jr., "*The Second Shepherd's Play:* A Reconsideration," *PMLA* 93, No. 1 (Jan 1978): 78-85.

Mâle, Emile, *The Gothic Image*, trans. Dora Nussey (New York: E. P. Dutton, 1913; reprint, New York: Harper Torchbook, 1958).

Malone, Kemp, C*hapters on Chaucer* (Baltimore: The Johns Hopkins Press, 1951).

Manly, John Matthews, ed., C*anterbury Tales by Geoffrey Chaucer* (New York: Henry Holt, [1928]).

———, *Some New Light on Chaucer* (New York: Henry Holt, [1926]; reprint, Gloucester, MA: Peter Smith, 1959).

Masefield, John, *Chaucer* (Cambridge, England: Cambridge University Press, 1931).

Meditations on the Life and Passion of Christ, ed. Charlotte D'Evelyn, EETS o.s. 158 (London: Oxford University Press, 1921).

The Middle Ages: A Concise Encyclopædia, ed. H. R. Loyn (1989; New York: Thames and Hudson, 1991 paperback).

Middle English Dictionary, ed. Hans Kurath and Sherman M. Kuhn, in progress (Ann Arbor, MI: University of Michigan Press, 1956-).

The Middle English Harrowing of Hell and the Gospel of Nicodemus, ed. William Henry Hulme, EETS o.s. 100 (London: Kegan Paul, Trench, Trübner and Co., 1907).

The Middle English Physiologus, ed. Hanneke Wirtjes, EETS o.s. 299 (Oxford: Oxford University Press, 1991).

Middleton, Anne, "The Idea of Poetry in the Reign of Richard II," *Speculum* 53 (Jan 1978): 94-114.

Miller, Robert P., "Allegory in the *Canterbury Tales*," in *Chaucer Criticism* I: The Canterbury Tales, ed. Richard Schoeck and Jerome

Taylor (Notre Dame, IN: University of Notre Dame Press, 1960).

Minto, William, *Characteristics of English Poets*, 2d. ed. (1874; London: William Blackwood and Sons, 1885).

Mirk, John, *Mirk's Festial: A Collection of Homilies*, ed. Theodor Erbe, EETS e.s. 96 (London: Kegan Paul, Trench, Trübner and Co., 1905).

Morey, Charles Rufus, *Mediaeval Art* (New York: W. W. Norton, 1942).

Muscatine, Charles, *Chaucer and the French Tradition* (Berkeley: University of California Press, 1957).

Oberman, Heiko A., "Fourteenth-Century Religious Thought: a Premature Profile," *Speculum* (Jan 1978): 80-93.

Owen, Charles A., Jr., *Pilgrimage and Storytelling in the* Canterbury Tales: *the Dialectic of "Ernest" and "Game"* (Norman, OK: University of Oklahoma Press, 1977).

Owst, Gerald R., *Literature and Pulpit in Medieval England: A Neglected Chapter in the History of English Letters and of the English People* (Cambridge, England: Cambridge University Press, 1933).

———, *Preaching in Medieval England: An Introduction to Sermons of the Period 1350–1450* (Cambridge, England: Cambridge University Press, 1926).

Oxford Dictionary of English Christian Names, ed. E. G. Withycombe, 2d rev. ed. (Oxford: Clarendon Press, 1977).

Page, Barbara, "Concerning the Host," *Chaucer Review* Vol. 4, 1 (1970): 1-13.

Pearsall, Derek, *The Times Higher Education Supplement*, quoted on cover of Kolve's *Imagery*.

Pecock, Reginald, *Reule of Crysten Religioun*, EETS o.s. 171 (London: Oxford University Press, 1927).

Robbins, Rossell Hope, "Popular Prayers in Middle English Verse," *Modern Philology* 36, No. 4 (May 1939): 337-49.

———, "Private Prayers in Middle English Verse," *Studies in Philology* 36 (July 1939): 466–75.

Robertson, D[urant] W[aite], Jr., *A Preface to Chaucer: Studies in Medieval Perspectives* (1962; Princeton, NJ: Princeton University Press, 1969 paperback).

——, *Chaucer's London* (New York: John Wiley and Sons, 1968; reprint, Ann Arbor, MI: UMI, 1992).

Rose, Martial, ed., *The Wakefield Mystery Plays* (New York: Doubleday, 1961; New York: W. W. Norton, 1969 paperback).

Rubin, Miri, *Corpus Christi: The Eucharist in Late Medieval Culture* (Cambridge, England: Cambridge University Press, 1991).

Ruskin, John, *The Works of John Ruskin*, ed. E.T. Cook and Alexander Wedderburn, 39 Vols. (New York: Longmans, Green, 1904).

Saintsbury, George, *A History of Criticism and Literary Taste in Europe*, 3 Vols. (New York: Dodd, Mead, 1900).

——, *The Flourishing of Romance and Rise of Allegory* (New York: Charles Scribner's Sons, 1897).

Skeat, Walter, *The Academy*, No. 1139 (3/23/1894).

——, ed., *The Complete Works of Geoffrey Chaucer*, 2d ed., 7 Vols. (1894-1897; Oxford: The Clarendon Press, 1900).

Speculum Christiani: A Middle English Treatise of the Fourteenth Century, ed. Gustaf Holmstedt, EETS o.s. 182 (London: Oxford University Press, 1933).

Speirs, John, *Chaucer the Maker* (London: Faber and Faber, 1951).

Spurgeon, Caroline F. E., ed., *Five Hundred Years of Chaucer Criticism and Allusion: 1357–1900* [Chaucer Society 1908–1917] 3 Vols. (New York: Cambridge University Press, 1925; New York: Russell and Russell, 1960).

The Stanzaic Life of Christ, ed. Frances A. Foster, EETS o.s. 166 (London: Oxford University Press, 1926).

Swann, Wim, *The Gothic Cathedral* (Garden City, NY: Doubleday, 1969).

The Tale of Beryn, ed. F. J. Furnivall and W. G. Stone, [Chaucer Society] Vol. 17 (London: N. Trübner and Co., 1887).

Tatlock, J.S.P., *The Mind and Art of Chaucer* (New York: Gordian Press, 1966).

———, and Arthur G. Kennedy, ed., *A Concordance to the Complete Works of Geoffrey Chaucer* (The Carnegie Institution of Washington, 1927; reprint, Gloucester, MA: Peter Smith, 1963).

Temko, Allan, *Notre Dame of Paris: the Biography of a Cathedral* (New York: Viking Press, 1952; Viking Compass, 1959).

ten Brink, Bernard, *History of English Literature*, trans. William Clarke Robinson, 2 Vols. (New York: Henry Holt, 1893).

Thynne, Francis, *Animadversions*, ed. G. H. Kingsley, rev. ed. F. J. Furnivall, EETS o.s. 9 (1865; rev. ed. London: Oxford University Press, 1875; reprint, 1965).

Towneley Plays, ed. George England and Alfred W. Pollard, EETS e.s. 71 (London: Kegan Paul, Trench, Trübner and Co., 1897).

Wakefield, Walter L. and Austin P. Evans, ed. and trans., *Heresies of the High Middle Ages* (New York: Columbia University Press, 1969).

Ward, Adolphus William, *Chaucer* (New York: Harper and Bros., [1887]).

Wickham, Glynne, *Early English Stages: 1300 to 1660*, 2 vols. in 3 (New York: Columbia University Press, 1959).

Wilson, R. M., *Early Middle English Literature*, 2d ed. (London: Methuen, 1951).

Withington, Robert, *English Pageantry: An Historical Outline*, 2 Vols. (Cambridge, MA: Harvard University Press, 1918-20; reprint, Benjamin Blom, 1963).

Wright, David, ed., *Geoffrey Chaucer: The Canterbury Tales* (Oxford: Oxford University Press, 1985).

Wright, Thomas, ed., *The Canterbury Tales,* [Percy Society 24, 25, 26] 3 Vols. (London: T. Richards, 1847).

Wyclif, John, *Selected English Works*, ed. Thomas Arnold, 3 Vols. (Oxford: Clarendon Press, 1869–71).

York Cycle of Mystery Plays, ed. J. S. Purvis (London: SPCK, [1957]).